Women of Achievement

Martha Stewart

Women of Achievement

Susan B. Anthony

Hillary Rodham Clinton

Marie Curie

Ellen DeGeneres

Nancy Pelosi

Rachael Ray

Eleanor Roosevelt

Martha Stewart

Women of Achievement

Martha Stewart

LIFESTYLE ENTREPRENEUR

Sherry Beck Paprocki

CHELSEA HOUSE
PUBLISHERS
An imprint of Infobase Publishing

MARTHA STEWART

Chelsea House
An imprint of Infobase Publishing
132 West 31st Street
New York NY 10001

Library of Congress Cataloging-in-Publication Data
Paprocki, Sherry Beck.
  Martha Stewart : Lifestyle Entrepreneur / Sherry Beck Paprocki.
    p. cm. — (Women of achievement)
  Includes bibliographical references and index.
  ISBN 978-1-60413-083-6 (hardcover : alk. paper) 1. Stewart, Martha. 2. Home economists—United States—Biography. 3. Businesswomen—United States—Biography. I. Title. II. Series.

  TX140.S74P37 2009
  640.92—dc22
  [B]
                                    2008034640

Chelsea House books are available at special discounts when purchased in bulk quantities for businesses, associations, institutions, or sales promotions. Please call our Special Sales Department in New York at (212) 967-8800 or (800) 322-8755.

You can find Chelsea House on the World Wide Web at http://www.chelseahouse.com

Series design by Erik Lindstrom
Cover design by Ben Peterson

Printed in the United States of America

Bang EJB 10 9 8 7 6 5 4 3 2 1

This book is printed on acid-free paper.

All links and Web addresses were checked and verified to be correct at the time of publication. Because of the dynamic nature of the Web, some addresses and links may have changed since publication and may no longer be valid.

CONTENTS

1	The Domestic Diva	7
2	A Big Family	16
3	A Model Woman	28
4	Perfectly Entertaining	40
5	Building an Omni-Business	55
6	A Powerful Force	64
7	A Different Kind of Home	75
8	Martha Stewart's Rebirth	96

Chronology	112
Notes	114
Bibliography	122
Further Resources	128
Picture Credits	129
Index	130
About the Author	135

The Domestic Diva

The green sprouts of new tulips at Martha Stewart's farm in Bedford, New York, are peeking through the soil. It is spring, and a rebirth of all things that Stewart loves is under way. Flowers are starting to blossom, animals are frolicking in the barnyard, new coops are being completed for the chickens, and a bluebird is plucking a fresh worm for a feast.

Stewart's blog on her Web site relates these pleasures of the new season, though she had still more reasons to cheer. On the first day of spring in 2008, she celebrated the completion of the 500th episode of her live television talk show—*The Martha Stewart Show*, which had debuted in 2005. A giant, 1,000-pound (454-kilogram) ice sculpture with the numerals 5-0-0 helped to mark the day.

Late-night talk-show host Conan O'Brien—on whose show Stewart had appeared just a few days before for St. Patrick's Day—danced around the studio kitchen with a sifter of gold glitter that he eventually put on a sparkling glazed ham. Laughing, Stewart reminded her viewers several times that the ham was now inedible. A little later in the show, former President Bill Clinton made a surprise appearance to congratulate Stewart, and he presented her with a basket that symbolizes friendship and was created by Rwandan women. At the end of the program, Stewart invited her entire staff onstage for a celebratory champagne toast with her and President Clinton.

Martha Stewart is, perhaps, the most successful housekeeper in the world. According to a profile of Stewart on Portfolio.com, her net worth is estimated to be $638 million.[1]

Stewart, though, did not always mingle with former presidents and celebrities. She was born in 1941, the second child in a family of six children, to parents of Polish descent. The cooking and gardening that she learned as a child at their home in New Jersey was integrated into her character at a very early age. Stories of Stewart's youth abound, partly because she focuses on childhood memories in her monthly glossy magazine, *Martha Stewart Living*. Still, Stewart was rare among women of that time—the vast majority of whom settled into marriages and family life and rarely looked for satisfaction beyond the home. Stewart, though, was different. She was a driven young woman who seemed to have more energy, ideas, and time than anyone else around her.

When she went to get her degree at Barnard College, which is now part of Columbia University, she initially thought she would be a schoolteacher. In college, she seemed to be following the path of so many others, as she put her life on hold to marry a man who was in law school. Soon after, though, she completed her degree and gave birth to her only child. Then she went on to a career as a stockbroker—one of the first women to work on Wall Street.[2]

Stewart's former Wall Street boss once talked about her outside interests, which would one day make his former employee a household name. "She did everything from raise dogs to breed hydrangeas to remodel a home—while she was leading the life of a full-time stockbroker. It was sort of amazing to watch," former boss Andy Monness told a writer from *Fortune* magazine.[3]

FROM CATERING TO ENTERTAINING

After six years on Wall Street, Stewart quit. She and her husband, Andy Stewart, purchased a historic house outside of New York City in the more rural community of Westport, Connecticut. Since her daughter, Alexis, was now in elementary school, she started a catering business out of her home to help at parties that her neighbors held. Of course, Stewart's ambitions did not end there. Through a retail shop, she sold food and entertainment kits that people could use at home.[4] Both the parties and the kits were so successful that Stewart's skills started to become legendary—not only for the way she cooked but also for the visual appeal that she brought to everything. She catered parties for people like noted designer and retailer Ralph Lauren as well as Paloma Picasso, who is the daughter of famed artist Pablo Picasso.[5] Soon after opening the store, Stewart wrote her first book, *Entertaining*.

It was in the early 1980s, after one of Stewart's catered parties, that an executive at Crown Publishing asked if she would be interested in writing the book. She and a small staff spent months gathering recipes, shooting photographs, and preparing the manuscript for a lifestyle book that was considered revolutionary at a time when housekeeping and cooking were seen as chores, rather than art.

Martha Stewart discussed her new book *Martha Stewart's Wedding Cakes* with *Today* show host Matt Lauer in January 2008. It had been more than 25 years since the publication of Stewart's first book, *Entertaining*—the tome that launched her vast lifestyle empire.

Chapters were written on topics like a tempura party for 16 people, a clambake for 30, and dessert parties for crowds of all sizes. Her recipes and style were a hit, and Stewart has never looked back.

She was thrilled to have the chance to produce an entire book about entertaining, one of her passions. "I really wanted to preserve all the memories and the delicious recipes that we created for all of those events,"[6] Stewart said about the book during an episode of *The Martha Stewart Show*. The show marked the twenty-fifth anniversary of the book's publication. While the audience sat at cocktail tables, Stewart reminisced about the early days of her career.

Since the release of *Entertaining* in 1982, Stewart's name has become a household reference signifying perfection in cooking, entertaining, gardening, decorating, and more. She has taught women—and men—myriad tricks to achieve domestic bliss. Whether it's braising lamb, cooking the perfect roast chicken, or creating healthy polenta cookies, Stewart has a knack for making delectable creations look and taste great. Whether she's focused on the tiny sprouts coming up in her gardens, planting the perfect container garden, or making crepe-paper flowers, she seems to know the way to accomplish excellence.

Just as she is known for her cooking and entertaining finesse, Stewart is also praised for her amazing craft ideas— finger-puppet cards, unusual tassel earrings, or custom-decorated Ugg boots, for example. She even has ideas for wrapping her creations in specially designed eco gift wrap, fancy cookie boxes, or cardboard cones that are ideal for candy.

As is apparent by all her achievements, Stewart is a woman who thrives on staying busy. "I rarely, rarely sit down and do nothing," she once confessed.[7] Through the years, Stewart has regularly said that she needs very little sleep, often getting by with only three hours a night. While building her empire, she has worked hard to stay ahead of household trends—trying to figure out how people will cook, what they will want to decorate with, and even what color of paint they will use in their homes.

To do this, her lifelong love of reading continues to be important. In the early days of her business, and still today, Stewart is an avid reader. She reads *The New York Times* and *The Wall Street Journal*, news magazines like *Time* and *Newsweek*, and books and book reviews.[8]

In addition, Stewart has learned to be a smart business-woman. For example, in 2008, she announced a deal that she had negotiated with Chef Emeril Lagasse. She purchased much of his business, including his kitchen gadgets, cookbooks, and television shows (but not his restaurants) for more than $45 million.[9] Obviously, Stewart is a master at creating partnerships. She has worked for more than two decades with Kmart and has an ongoing relationship with the department store Macy's, where she has more recently introduced dishes, linens, and other products.

BUILDING THE BRAND

After the publication of *Entertaining* in 1982, Stewart's career took off. She wrote more books as her name became synonymous with the best in cooking, crafting, and entertaining. She wrote articles for *The New York Times* and was a columnist for the magazine *House Beautiful*. She produced television specials about lifestyle and CDs that featured dinner music.[10] At one point, she garnered $10,000 for lectures she gave to fans and charged $900 a person for her followers to attend seminars at her Connecticut home. Everyone, it seemed, wanted to learn about homemaking from the expert. Indeed, the queen of domesticity was building a

DID YOU KNOW?

Not only does Martha Stewart sleep for only a few hours, she also has been known to keep her light on all night. That way, if she wakes up, she can immediately start to read or do work. As one friend told a reporter from *The New York Times*, "It sounds obsessive, but it's not. It's just Martha's determination not to waste time."

During the 1980s, as Martha Stewart's popularity began to grow, she held seminars on entertaining at her home in Connecticut. Here, some of her students surrounded her, admiring a table full of her creations.

huge brand—a brand that would make her name familiar to nearly all Americans.

In 1990, Stewart launched her own magazine, *Martha Stewart Living*, and a few years later she added her first television series. The TV show, with the same name as her magazine, was produced and taped at her historic 1805 Connecticut estate. The home's fruit orchards, gardens, pool, barn, and perfectly decorated rooms provided a lush setting for a homemaking program. Stewart thrived in its environment, even displaying her exotic Araucana chickens and their pastel blue eggs. "We could never duplicate this place as a (television) set," the show's executive producer, Leslie McNeil, once told a reporter from *The New York Times*.[11]

Stewart's creative vision has led to much of her success. Not only is she concerned with how something tastes, but she also knows how to create awe-inspiring dishes, table settings, crafts, gifts, and more. Certainly, Stewart's deep knowledge of business as well as her passion about home style has made her business grow. But, she says, her fans' enthusiasm about lifestyle and family developed at the same time.

She once speculated that, during the 1980s, television viewers were enthralled with the luxury lifestyles seen on shows like *Dallas* and *Dynasty*. When she started to do *Martha Stewart Living*, Stewart set out to show others how to create the perfect life in a rather ordinary setting. "People were living vicariously through them," she said of these TV shows that glamorized excessive wealth and all of the extravagances that came along with it. "I think my approach is so much more simple and so much nicer a lifestyle. People understand."[12]

As Stewart's popularity grew, so did the criticism that surrounded her seemingly perfect brand. For some, Stewart became the brunt of jokes and sarcastic humor. Still, for every person who did not like Stewart, there were many more who celebrated her success and eagerly awaited her next idea.

Despite her accomplishments, Stewart has gone through horribly troubling times, too. After many years of marriage, she and her husband divorced. Then, in 2002, her dealings in the stock market led to a federal investigation. In the end, charges regarding her stock trading were dropped, but Stewart was found guilty on four major charges dealing with misleading investigators and obstructing justice. She was sent to prison. Stewart, the domestic maven who had built an empire worth hundreds of millions of dollars, was housed in a federal women's penitentiary in West Virginia, where she bunked with other inmates for five months in late 2004 and early 2005.

For many people, such a turn of events would be devastating. A once extremely successful woman, who was deeply admired for her creative work, was now in jail. Many observers predicted that this would be the end of the Martha Stewart empire. Others continued to defend her, based on her success and resourcefulness. "This is a woman who, if pressed, could twist a prison spoon and a Cheetos wrapper into a cheerful centerpiece," writer Virginia Heffernan commented on the Web site *Slate*.[13]

It turns out that Heffernan was right and Stewart's detractors were wrong. Stewart made friends while in prison and learned about ingredients, cooking styles, and lifestyles that she had never known before. Her strong work ethic also saw her through these difficult times. Although the value of her company decreased while she was incarcerated, Stewart emerged from prison with a new outlook on how she would approach the world again.

Stewart went right back to work. In fact, it seems that she never stopped thinking up new ideas even while in prison. Soon after she was out, her new, live daytime talk show debuted. She started to buy brands, like the one belonging to Lagasse, and worked on her partnership with Macy's while forming another with a homebuilder called KB Home. Despite the setback, Stewart was moving forward with her career and her passions.

Apparently, she was not willing to shelve more than 25 years of domestic success. Stewart may have had a personal rebirth after spending time in prison. Today her life appears to be reflective of everything she loves about springtime. As she told one of her television audiences, that involves renewal, regeneration, and rebirth.

A Big Family

Martha Helen Kostyra was born on August 3, 1941, to Eddie and Martha Kostyra. She was the second in a family of six children and the first daughter; her older brother, Eric, was three when she was born. Martha would grow up with a new sibling born every three years or so. First came Frank, then Kathy, George, and the baby of the family, Laura.

The Kostyra family was a middle-class, Catholic family whose Polish heritage was always present. Eddie Kostyra was a pharmaceutical sales representative, and his wife—once all of the children were in school—became a teacher. At first, they lived in the industrial city of Jersey City, but when Martha was three, the Kostyra family moved to a small, neat home in the town of Nutley, New Jersey.

The house was at 86 Elm Place—a location that Stewart sometimes still mentions on her television show or in her magazine.[1] "The kitchen was very basic when we first moved to Elm Place," Stewart recalled in her magazine a few years ago. "There was a stove, a refrigerator, a worktable, and an eating nook; the large enamel sink was low, and Mother complained about leaning over it to wash dishes and pots and pans. When the new kitchen was constructed, there were miraculous new counters, a dishwasher, a wall oven, a gas four-burner cooktop, and a double sink at a sensible height."[2]

When the family first moved into the home, many hours were spent in the breakfast nook, where a family friend had painted scenes from Walt Disney cartoons. Besides eating breakfast here, the Kostyra children could frequently be found in the nook doing homework after supper. For a short time, the family had a pet, a fox terrier named Shiner.[3]

LEARNING FROM HER PARENTS

Stewart's mother cooked and sewed clothes for her family—skills that Martha easily learned as she helped out after her siblings were born. Martha's mother, whom she referred to as Big Martha for many years, was born to a Polish family in Buffalo, New York, in 1914. She grew up to be an expert cook and housekeeper by the time she gave birth to her children, and her fond childhood memories of making cakes, pies, and other specialties helped her re-create them in her own kitchen. Eventually, her recipes and techniques were passed on to her children.

Martha's father was an enthusiastic gardener who was happy to relay his expertise to his oldest daughter, and she happily soaked up the knowledge. Martha started to work with her father in his garden from the time she was about

In December 2003, Martha Stewart appeared on *Larry King Live* with her mother, Martha Kostyra *(right)*. Stewart learned about cooking and sewing from her mother while she was growing up, and Stewart's father, Eddie Kostyra, passed on his love of gardening to his daughter.

three years old, helping with the tomatoes, carrots, string beans, and figs that he grew there. "Our garden on Elm Place in Nutley was organic," Stewart once reported in her magazine, "the soil enriched with composted everything, even the heads and innards of the many, many fish that Dad caught in the ocean and lakes and cleaned right into the tomato patch."[4]

Stewart learned the art of working in the wild from her older brother, Eric. "It was he who taught me to shoot, to trap, to tie flies, and to fish," she wrote in her 1988 book *Martha Stewart's Quick Cook Menus*. "Although I do not hunt to kill, I do still fish—and there are few things I like better than freshly caught trout simply cooked in a pan."[5]

The Kostyra family ate well and enjoyed the various dishes created from fresh garden produce in their mother's kitchen. Eddie Kostyra traveled to New York City frequently on business and would often bring back spices and fruits from various ethnic grocers, which encouraged the Kostyra children to be rather adventuresome in their tastes.[6] Stewart remembers that once, when she was six or seven years old, her father came home with a paper sack containing six red fruits, which he called Chinese apples.[7]

Yet, one of the family's favorite meals included their mother's homemade pierogi, a Polish dish featuring pastry dough stuffed with potatoes and cheese. "I have eaten 27 of them at one sitting," Stewart once proudly proclaimed.[8]

While growing up, Stewart shared a bedroom with her sister Kathy. They shared a mahogany bed with a firm mattress—information that Stewart relayed in one of her "Remembering" columns in her magazine. The column mainly discussed the firmness of mattresses in Stewart's life and how she was influenced by her father's belief that an extra-firm mattress would lead to good posture and good health. It was a practice, Stewart said, that she followed even into adulthood when purchasing her own mattresses.[9]

IN HER OWN WORDS

In her first book, *Entertaining* (1982), Martha Stewart wrote about the childhood foods that influenced her:

> My early memories are bound up with mushroom soup and pierogi.

The children were taught a strong work ethic and always had chores that they did to contribute to the household. Young Martha's skills were honed in cooking, gardening and sewing—not as hobbies but as ways to help her family. Stewart's parents had lived through the Great Depression, and they believed in following a strict financial budget for their household to ensure that their young children would have food and clothing. There was an expectation that the children would correctly do their chores in a timely fashion or their parents would start to ask questions. The Kostyras were known to be strict and disciplined parents, and they had high expectations for their children. The family was fairly religious—like most Catholics at that time, they did not eat meat on Fridays.

From the time Martha was about 10 years old, she spent two weeks each summer with her maternal grandparents, Polish immigrants who lived several hours away in Buffalo, New York. Martha's grandmother taught her the fine art of preserving and canning various foods, making jellies and jams, and other cooking techniques. Her grandfather was an ironworker who designed fancy handrails and other architectural detailing for churches and office buildings.[10] Perhaps it was spending time with her grandfather that also led to Stewart's keen interest in design and construction projects for her homes.

THE EARLY CATERER

In her book *Entertaining*, Stewart acknowledged that she planned birthday parties for the neighborhood children for fun. She also planned these parties because they paid more than baby-sitting paid at 50 cents an hour. So, even as a youngster, Martha had figured out how to earn money while doing something she enjoyed.[11] Nonetheless, Martha also baby-sat while she was a teenager, and she would often spend her baby-sitting money on patterns or skeins of wool so that she could knit a scarf or mittens—activities Stewart considered very special. "When I was a child, embroidery, sewing, knitting, crocheting, and tatting skills were part of growing up," she said. "Every birthday and holiday, I received a kit for one or more of these crafts."[12]

Holidays in the Kostyra household were times for celebrating family traditions. "Christmas Eve was always a very holy day for us; it was strictly a meatless repast, and we always introduced the meal by breaking the holy bread," said Stewart's mother, who appeared on her holiday special *Christmas from Martha's Home* in 2002.[13] Among other special Christmas treats, the family always had a box full of cookie twists, called *chrusciki*, which were fried in oil and then dusted with powdered sugar on top. "I can't have Christmas without them," Stewart once said in her magazine.[14]

As a child, Martha was an excellent student who loved to read. When her chores were finished, she had a favorite reading chair, where she would plop down to relax and pick up a book. Sometimes, she would take a book outside and sit in her favorite tree to read. "On Sunday mornings, because we had such chaos in our house, everybody running around and getting dressed to go to church and everything, I sat in the car and read," she said. "I read everything."[15]

"In third grade I won the contest at the public library for being able to get a score of a hundred on a reading test," she once recalled. "The reading test was based on the numbers of books you read, and the amount that you retain from those books."[16] Stewart said that she was the first child to pass the test and, thus, was allowed to go into the adult Stockton Room at the local library—a room that was named after the author Frank Stockton.[17] Even as a youngster, Martha was reading the adult biographies of United States presidents, famed author Harriet Beecher Stowe, and others.

"And as I read all of the classics, what remained most vivid in my memory were the banquet scenes in Sir Walter Scott, the Roman punch dinners in Edith Wharton novels, and the country weekends in Tolstoy's *Anna Karenina*," she wrote in her first book, *Entertaining*. "Entertaining always seemed natural to me, a matter of taking something very appealing to me—a favorite dish, a holiday, an activity—and making it bigger, to include others."[18]

Martha's love of learning led her initially to want to be a teacher, which was a common career choice for women of that time. She was inspired by a couple of her own elementary school teachers, and she thought she would eventually go to college to get a teaching degree. At the same time that she was considering her future, she was also developing a penchant for doing her household chores in a correct manner so that the clothes would fit and the food would always be tasty. Never did Martha likely dream that the job for which she would become famous would be one in which she taught people how to cook, sew, create crafts, and build small projects.

"A woman who made her own dresses throughout high school understands not just the pride in the craftsmanship but the importance of doing the job right the first time," wrote Mary Elizabeth Williams on the Web site *Salon*.[19] Indeed, Martha Stewart was a woman who valued domesticity and learned how to do it correctly before she even graduated from high school.

Stewart—a tall young woman with an all-American look—started to model before she was out of high school. Although she was not considered a supermodel by today's standards, her work helped her pay to attend a small college called Barnard in nearby New York City. "I applied at some nice colleges (including) Stanford, and then I realized, I can't go to Stanford; it's across the country!" Stewart once said to Oprah Winfrey during an interview.

Martha Kostyra is seen in a photograph that appeared in February 1959 in Nutley High School's *Maroon and Gray* newspaper. Martha had started to model before she was out of high school. She used the money she earned from modeling to help with expenses at Barnard College in New York City.

"I didn't have enough money to go away, though I'd love to know what my life would be like if I'd gone to Stanford."[20]

ON TO COLLEGE

That's why Stewart decided to attend Barnard, which was closer to her family home. It was less expensive to travel

JULIA CHILD

During her lifetime, Julia Child was one of the most famous chefs in the world. She was a celebrity largely because of her television shows and her many books. She was also popular because of her personality. Child was funny and explained fancy dishes in a way that made them easy to understand. She is credited with changing the way Americans think about food, especially French cooking.

Child was born on August 15, 1912, in Pasadena, California, as Julia McWilliams. Raised in an affluent family, she did not spend much time in the kitchen because the family had a cook. Instead, she played tennis, wrote and performed plays, and sometimes got into trouble for smoking her dad's cigars.

Child attended Smith College in Massachusetts and was a member of the women's basketball team. A few years after her graduation, World War II broke out and she moved to Washington, D.C., to work for the Office of Strategic Services (which was later replaced by the Central Intelligence Agency). In time, she took a post overseas, in Ceylon, an island off India that is known today as Sri Lanka. She was one of the few women there. Her job involved working with secret documents. Later, after being shipped to China in 1945, she met Paul Child, a fellow OSS employee.

When the war ended, Paul and Julia returned to the United States and married. Soon, they were overseas again. In 1948, Paul's job with the U.S. government took him to the American Embassy in Paris. Thanks in part to her husband's love of food, there, and it was a good school. Stewart also won a partial scholarship that helped pay for her tuition. While attending Barnard, Stewart was named one of *Glamour* magazine's

along with France's fabulous cuisine, Child sought to learn more about how to prepare meals. At 37, she attended the famous Le Cordon Bleu cooking school as the only female student in the class. She and two friends then formed their own cooking school and, after 10 years of working on it, published a book in 1961 called *Mastering the Art of French Cooking*. It was a big book featuring 800 pages, and it became a big hit. For many years, the book was credited with making it easier for Americans without formal training to make complex French recipes.

After the Childs had moved to Cambridge, Massachusetts, Julia was invited to appear on a Boston public broadcasting TV program in 1962 to promote her book. Instead of just talking about her recipes, she actually prepared an omelet, which was considered to be a fancy dish at the time, and she did so with showmanship, enthusiasm, and humor. The audience loved her, and she was invited to host her own show. *The French Chef* became a smash hit and earned major awards.

Child's show launched a long public career as a celebrity chef: She appeared regularly on such national television programs as *Good Morning America* and numerous TV specials, and she published several more acclaimed cookbooks.

In 1993, she became the first woman inducted into the Culinary Institute Hall of Fame, and France recognized her with its highest honor, the Legion d'Honneur, in 2000.

Child died on August 13, 2004, at the age of 91 at her home in Santa Barbara, California.

Best-Dressed College Girls in 1961.[21] In the meantime, she began to reconsider her original plans to become a teacher. She was excited about some of the other career opportunities that she was introduced to during her coursework.

"In college I discovered the world of chemistry, which I loved. I discovered the world of architectural history. I discovered so many different things that I decided that maybe I would forgo the teaching career for a while," she said.[22]

After two years of college, though, Stewart took a slight break. She married Andy Stewart, a law student with whom she had fallen in love. Apparently, Andy Stewart knew how to work his way into his girlfriend's heart. On their second date, he took her to a Balkan/Armenian restaurant in New York City. In one of her later cookbooks, Stewart fondly recalled the wonderful beef and lamb shish kabobs that she sampled. It was that evening that Stewart decided that she must eventually travel to Greece, Turkey, and Yugoslavia, where such dishes were common.[23]

One of the first formal dinner parties that Stewart recalls was hosted by Andy's sister as they celebrated their engagement, she wrote in the book *Entertaining*. Andy's sister served roasted chicken, corn on the cob, and chocolate cake. The table featured real cloths, and candles were burning.[24] Soon after, in July 1961, Andy Stewart and Martha Kostyra were married in St. Paul's Chapel on the campus of Columbia University. Martha's dress was one that she and her mother made out of embroidered Swiss organdy, which they had purchased at a store in New York City.[25]

For their honeymoon, they took what would be Martha's first trip to Europe—a trip that also greatly influenced her culinary interests in diverse dishes and methods of preparation. Once home in New York, she was enthralled with a chef by the name of Julia Child who had produced a book called *Mastering the Art of French Cooking*. In her free time, Stewart visited many of the city's finest restaurants and, when possible, talked with chefs about the dishes they prepared.

Eventually, Martha and Andy Stewart traveled more. One trip took them to Greece, Turkey, and Yugoslavia. Stewart came back well-versed in the art of creating the perfect beef and lamb shish kabob.

Even though Stewart was developing a keen interest in varied ethnic cooking techniques, she continued her education at Barnard, eventually getting a degree in European and architectural history. She still modeled as well, doing work for products like Breck and Clairol shampoos, Lifebuoy soap, and Tareyton cigarettes.[26] But after the birth of Alexis in 1965, Stewart ended her modeling career.

Little did she know at that time that she would be in the spotlight for much of the rest of her life.

A Model Woman

In 1967, Martha Stewart started a career as a stockbroker. With her daughter now two years old, she thought it was time to get a job. Stewart's father-in-law was an investment banker, and she was intrigued with being part of Wall Street. Even though she had no experience working in the stock market, Stewart jumped into her new career with complete enthusiasm.

"It was a time when there were very few women on Wall Street," said Andy Monness, the man who hired her. "She was beautiful, she was Columbia-educated, and it looked as if she was going to work very hard because she was from a poor background. She seemed like a good package to bet on."[1]

Stewart's family wasn't exactly poor, but with six children to feed, her parents had to work very hard. The strong work ethic that they instilled in their children—with their daily list of chores and get-it-done attitude—was all it took to create a hard-working daughter who was confident that she could accomplish any challenge presented to her.

Stewart got along well with her co-workers on Wall Street. "I would say her strongest attribute, other than being intelligent, was that everyone liked her," Monness said many years after Stewart had left the firm.[2]

Yet, there were some aspects of Wall Street that Stewart did not much care for. For example, the men always wore stodgy suits. As a woman and a former model, Stewart enjoyed dressing differently from most of her peers. "I wore hot pants," she told two friends many years later, referring to the very short shorts that were popular at the time. "I thought the way of dressing there was just stupid. I had beautiful long legs. I wore brown velvet hot pants with brown stockings and high heels."[3]

Certainly, for that reason and others, Stewart was probably a standout during her years as a stockbroker. At the time, the Stewarts lived in a small apartment in the midst of the city, but Stewart's homemaking skills were not dampened—she grew herbs and flowers indoors and worked hard to make a good home. On the weekends, the young family would travel to Massachusetts, where they had a small getaway retreat. But Stewart's desire for the country life was not sated. After working on Wall Street for six years, she decided to quit.

"When I got married and had a child and went to work, my day was all day, all night. You lose your sense of balance," she said more than 20 years later. "That was in the late '60s, '70s, women went to work, they went crazy. They thought the workplace was more exciting than the home. They thought the family could wait. … The family can't wait. And women have found that out."[4]

Apparently, Stewart had a desire to do more creative work that would require her special touch. Even though she had a busy job for six years, she had continued cooking and homemaking in the manner in which she had been taught during her childhood. Her love of gardening, cooking, and eating wonderful food had not diminished. Even while busy on Wall Street, the tastes and aromas of great dishes stuck with her. In one of her books, in fact, she referred to a Greenwich Village restaurant that she would visit while living and working in the city that made a delectable recipe with mussels.[5] Indeed, Stewart's arsenal of cooking prowess was being enhanced no matter where she was and what she was doing.

LEAVING THE CITY

While Stewart was still working on Wall Street, she and Andy began to look at homes outside of New York City. Eventually they decided to buy an old farmhouse in West-port, Connecticut, that had been a rental property for many years. The dilapidated, historic house was set on two acres; many years earlier, the property had been an onion farm.[6]

At the time, Westport was a fairly quiet town that was mainly inhabited by professionals—lawyers, writers, adver-tising executives and artists—who commuted to work in nearby New York. It was the kind of town that nurtured creativity and free thought among its residents, who were extremely motivated and hard-working. Thus, when the Stewarts bought their farmhouse, they seemed to be the perfect fit.

Stewart immediately knew that the rundown house could be refurbished into a wonderful home for her fam-ily. Instinctively, she knew that the barren land that had only a few trees on it could be turned into lush, wonderful gardens. She could visualize a renovated interior that was polished and gleaming instead of the dilapidated property that they had purchased. Despite all of the work involved, the Stewarts plunged into a country life. And, in true Martha Stewart style, no project would be small. The first task was planting an orchard. Then, they built a two-story garage and installed a pool. The projects continued for many years.[7]

Martha and Andy Stewart poured hours of their time into the renovation of the home they began to refer to as Turkey Hill, since its address was 48 Turkey Hill Road South. Martha quit her city job in 1973 and moved with the family into their new homestead, although Andy kept working for a publishing company that was based in New York City. At the time, Martha Stewart had grand visions for what her home would be. As a surprise for Andy one Father's Day, she purchased a dismantled barn and had it shipped to Turkey Hill, where they rebuilt it.[8] The Stewarts started to raise chickens, turkeys, and sheep. Massive gardens were planted, and landscapes were perfected.

In the Stewarts' early days at Turkey Hill, Martha went about furnishing the home with rare finds from local flea markets and antique shops. She began to accumulate an expansive collection of framed mirrors, glistening chandeliers, and antique furnishings. She changed paint colors from room to room, creating various settings and different room designs as though it were an ongoing hobby. However, no one—including Martha Stewart— seemed to know what would happen at Turkey Hill in the coming years.

BEYOND RENOVATIONS

The massive renovation and restoration of Turkey Hill took up much of the Stewarts' time, but Martha had other ambitions, too. She gave cooking lessons to little Alexis and some of her friends. One day, she instinctively put an advertisement in a local newspaper. She had decided to open a catering business, based out of her home, with a friend from her college years. Even though the partnership was short-lived, the local community welcomed Stewart's services and she began to plan wonderful dinners and parties that made her the idol of many of her customers.

Filled with baskets and pots and pans that hung from the ceiling, Stewart's kitchen at Turkey Hill took on epic

TURKEY HILL

For more than 30 years, Martha Stewart owned Turkey Hill, her home in Westport, Connecticut, near the Long Island Sound. The residence, named after the street on which it is located, Turkey Hill Road South, was a rundown farmhouse when she and Andy Stewart bought it in 1971. She described the place in an article in *Martha Stewart Living* as suffering from neglect. "There was not much of a kitchen and no usable bathroom," she said. "The basement was damp, and there was no porch, terrace, garden, or driveway."*

But the house had appeal—good bones, she wrote—and so they paid $46,750 for it. Three years later, the Stewarts bought a two-acre parcel of land south of the original property. Over time, Stewart added a barn, a chicken coop, a garden shed, a swimming pool, and a garage. Massive landscaping took place, with bulldozers reshaping the ground. She began to appreciate the impact of stone in landscaping, either as a wall or a fireplace. She would fly over her property and see her mistakes in how she laid out her gardens and plantings. After such observations, she would move trees and hedges to make things just right. Her property was a proportions. There, the busy woman cooked up meals for hordes of clients. She kept all the ingredients close at hand—various types of eggs, spices, and fresh produce. A table, set in front of the fireplace, made a cozy space in which to entertain family and close friends. Counter space was limited, so a thick butcher-block table that Stewart had received from a beloved uncle, a butcher in New Jersey, provided more space on which to work.

gardener's delight, with a mix of magnolia trees, climbing roses, and vegetable gardens.

Turkey Hill played a big part in Stewart's business because she used it on her TV programs and in photographs for her books. In addition, her work on the house and in the garden gave her many ideas to write and talk about. In 2006, Stewart put the colonial-style farmhouse estate up for sale. One Web site described it as: "Just over 3,100-sq. feet and is situated on 4 acres of beautifully landscaped grounds (would you expect anything less from Martha Stewart?). . . . The 3-bedroom, 2-bath house was originally built in 1805. It was maintained in excellent condition and features central air, a full walk-out basement and a heated pool."** Stewart's price tag was $8,995,000.

A year later, it sold for considerably less than what she wanted: $6.7 million.

---

*Martha Stewart, "Remembering Turkey Hill," *Martha Stewart Living*. October 2007.
**Nicole Weston, "Martha Stewart's Farmhouse for Sale," *Luxist*. June 5, 2006.

Martha Stewart kneaded dough in August 1976 in the kitchen at Turkey Hill, her home in Westport, Connecticut. In the mid-1970s, Stewart started to run a catering business from her home. In short time, her services for dinners and parties were much in demand.

Following one very successful dinner party that Stewart catered, she was approached about writing her first book. She was thrilled, though somewhat overwhelmed, by the idea. Nonetheless, she had all of the skills needed to organize a fabulous event, so a writing career based on her entertaining experience was launched. Eventually, Stewart adopted the mud room at Turkey Hill as her home office, producing dozens more books there.

Entertaining was the perfect topic for that first publication. From the time she was a child putting on birthday parties for friends, Stewart always saw parties as dramatic productions. A dinner would be nothing, she had decided, if it did not include some drama along the way. Thus, various themes emerged at her events, as did the protocol of what to prepare and how to serve it. In her first book, Stewart discussed everything from the dishes served, to creating the right atmosphere with music and furnishings, to selecting the people for the guest list. For example, she said, she always includes one extrovert who can keep the conversation going while the cook is busy.

Certainly, in the early days of her catering business, Stewart made plenty of mistakes—such as watching the icing on a wedding cake melt away in the summertime heat. Another time, she learned that lighting was important, as she watched guests try to see the food being served at an outdoor buffet after it was dark. Her expertise evolved over the years, though, and her events and dinners became more successful, one right after the next. "I remember when I first met Martha, years ago at a party. She lit up the room," billionaire developer Donald Trump once wrote in *Time* magazine. "Before I even knew who she was, it was obvious that this was someone special."9

Once *Entertaining* was published in 1982, it seemed that readers were hungry for the education that Stewart presented. Even though she had never become a teacher, Stewart was suddenly put in the role of teaching thousands of readers. The tips and hints in her first book were well received, and it seemed that Stewart's reputation as an expert on entertaining was sealed.

Stewart's life became extremely busy, with additional clients to serve and events to plan. And, it seemed, her desire to create the perfect meals and the perfect events led some people to shy away from working with her. As Stewart's popularity grew, so did her reputation for being a controlling perfectionist. But, as Stewart knew from her childhood, if directions were not followed and deadlines were not met, then an event could potentially be a big flop.

BRANCHING OUT

In the meantime, Stewart's instincts about running a business also seemed superb. In 1987, Stewart signed a five-year contract with Kmart to be its national spokes-woman and a lifestyle and home-entertaining consultant. She would also design products for bed, bath, and table-top. When Kmart wanted her to make a deal with the Lifetime cable network that would more broadly promote her books, Stewart refused, much to the regret of store officials. She surprised them when she got a better deal that allowed her to appear regularly on the *Today* show, the mainstream morning program with a bigger audience. "She fought tooth and nail for what her image would be like," one Kmart consultant said. "And she often won because she was right."[10]

By this time, Stewart's book-writing career was well established. After the noted popularity of *Entertaining*, her writing career went into high gear. Her next book, *Martha Stewart's Quick Cook* (1983), was based on recipes from a monthly column she had started to write for *House Beautiful* magazine. *Hors d'Oeurves*, featuring only appetizers, was released in 1984. *Pie and Tarts* came out in 1985, and two years later, she released another favorite, *Weddings*. By then, 340,000 copies of *Entertaining* had been sold, and Stewart was officially considered an authority.[11]

Weddings, it seems, changed the style in which weddings of the time were being celebrated. "Judging from the book, the days of the barefoot wedding on the mountaintop are over," wrote a reporter for *The New York Times*.[12] For Stewart, though, the book had been under way for a long time.

For more than three years, Stewart had overseen the catering, the writing, and the photographing of weddings

Martha Stewart and her friend, restaurant consultant Ruth Leserman, chopped mushrooms while preparing a luncheon in 1982 to celebrate the publication of Stewart's first book, *Entertaining*. That venture was just the start—Stewart published four more books over the next five years.

that were pictured and discussed in the book. But not all of the events in the book were completely planned. One weekend, Stewart was driving by a wedding in Martha's Vineyard and discovered that the bride and some of her family members were trying to re-create Stewart's basket-weave cake that had been portrayed in *Entertaining*. A delighted Stewart offered to finish decorating the cake, if the family permitted her to take photographs during the reception that she could print in *Weddings*. The family easily agreed.

A LIFESTYLE GURU

Situations such as this one offered clues to Stewart's growing popularity. People around the country were not only trying her recipes; they were attempting to re-create the events and the drama that Stewart infused in her books. Her passion for entertaining translated well into words. She began to see herself as a guru of sorts, someone who was happy to share her innate knowledge with an increasing number of fans. "I am a commitment to a kind of lifestyle, that's what I am," she told a reporter for *The New York Times* in 1987.[13]

Stewart wrote still more books. As *Weddings* was rolling off the presses, she was putting together a book called *The Wedding Planner*. In addition, she moved forward with a book called *Quick Cook Menus*, which was published in 1988. By then, Stewart's recipes and decorating ideas were becoming reflective of a lifestyle change across the United States. "*Quick Cook Menus* is not just about food, not even just about entertaining," said the brief copy on the inside flap of the book. "It's about a way of life—gracious, enjoyable, and accessible."[14]

One of the menus in the book featured smoked chicken and noodle salad, spicy sweet-and-sour cabbage, and tangerine sorbet. Stewart credited her daughter, Alexis, with inspiring her to create Asian dishes. By the late 1980s, Alexis had grown into a young woman with her own tastes and interests; she had graduated high school and gone off to college at her mother's alma mater, Barnard. "Alexis has taught me one secret to Oriental cooking: you must have the right ingredients," Stewart wrote in *Quick Cook Menus*.[15]

By this time, Stewart had met many of the famous chefs of the time: Paul Prudhomme, known for his famed New Orleans restaurant called K-Paul's Louisiana Kitchen, introduced her to Louisiana sausages, which she immediately loved. She traveled far and wide, both publicizing her books and focusing on regional foods. In Paris, she was introduced to a dish called ratatouille, which included a combination of fresh vegetables like zucchini, peppers, onions, eggplant, and tomatoes seasoned with garlic, thyme, and marjoram and cooked in olive oil. She wrote of the herbs and olive oil she found in Tuscany, Italy.

Certainly, as Stewart was building her empire, she was having a lot of fun along the way. Food, it seemed, was her passion. With her ability to create recipes and decorate with finesse, she had attracted a huge following. Her regular appearances on *Today* and guest appearances on other television programs added to her national prominence. Journalists from around the country began to write about her successes and shortcomings. "Is the cult of the domestic goddess making a comeback—with entertainment guru Martha Stewart its high priestess?" asked one writer for *USA Today*.[16] Certainly, no other women in recent years had made the impact on homemaking that Stewart had.

Perfectly Entertaining

Martha Stewart's catering business in the 1980s was growing in popularity so much that Martha, herself, was in demand. Despite the success of her books, her fans and followers wanted to learn directly from her. About once a month, she started to offer seminars on entertaining at her Turkey Hill home. There, she would introduce various foods and recipes that were not yet common to American households. One such dish was seafood risotto, in which she marinated fresh seafood in citrus, sautéed it, and served it with a specially prepared type of rice called risotto.

Certainly, Stewart's cooking skills were all the rage. But, beyond her culinary prowess, Stewart had other ideas, too. She collected fabrics from tag sales and flea markets and set up provocative designs for the dining room table and other areas of the home.

The upkeep and refurbishment at Turkey Hill continued to keep Stewart and her husband busy, too. They had purchased additional property adjacent to Turkey Hill on which they planted extensive gardens. The property's sloping land ended at a nearby river, which flowed into the Long Island Sound. Stewart greatly appreciated the expansive gardens, along with the peacefulness that the property offered when she sought solace from her very busy days.

But even though her business was growing, Stewart's personal life was headed for a crash. After she returned home from a book tour in 1987, her husband told her that he was leaving her. By all accounts, Stewart was extremely upset by his announcement and struggled to deal with Andy's departure from Turkey Hill.[1] They had been married for 26 years, and Stewart thought that she had found her companion for life. Alexis had grown up and gone off to college, so only the two of them were at home most of the time. Eventually, though, the couple divorced. After her husband left, Stewart continued to live at the Westport homestead with two cats, named Teeny and Weeny.[2]

Stewart's passion for homemaking seemed undiminished by her husband's departure. By 1989, she had produced 45 commercials for Kmart and sold 2.5 million books that focused on food and entertaining. That year, a Christmas special was set at Turkey Hill, complete with fake snow since it was taped months before, when the weather was still somewhat warm.

By this point, Stewart's seventh book, called *Martha Stewart's Christmas*, was ranked number two among best sellers on the *New York Times* list of advice books. Stewart shared her own holiday traditions in the book, including

Martha and Andy Stewart posed in April 1987 in the garden outside their home at Turkey Hill in Connecticut. Although the Stewarts were smiling in this photograph, times were not terribly happy at Turkey Hill. Soon after, Andy Stewart announced that he was leaving Martha.

cooking 300 plum puddings for family and friends each year as well as decorating her own wrapping paper. Even though Stewart admitted to working more than anyone else she knew, she just seemed unable to stop, *and* she seemed to enjoy every minute of it. "I don't sleep and I'm tired lots of times, but I still will take the time to gild a pumpkin, to marbleize a Christmas ornament," she once told a reporter. "I do it because I really like to do it."[3]

Despite all of her energy and good works, people began to look at Stewart as though she were too perfect. *Spy* magazine featured her among a list of people most hated by peers in the food industry. Some people started to say that Stewart stole recipes and revised them into her own versions, taking all the credit. But, the kitchen maven rebutted that thought. "I don't consciously go and plagiarize people's work," Stewart said when asked by a *USA Today* reporter.[4] In fact, in most of her cookbooks, she gives extensive credit to friends, neighbors, employees, and family members for their recipes and assistance.

Despite what naysayers reported, it seemed that Stewart intuitively knew that her readers were much like her. They liked to stay busy, and they liked the kinds of projects that she created for them—whether it was a great recipe such as smoked chicken and noodle salad or a fun craft such as baking and erecting the pieces of a gingerbread house. She was now 48, but the sleep she lost while engaged in a project of passion seemed to go unnoticed. She continued to stay thin, and her blond hair beautifully framed her friendly face. Still, she was a taskmaster for those who worked with her—encouraging all to be as perfect as possible in what they set out to accomplish. By now Stewart needed a staff to assist her with the projects and creations that she developed. Stewart saw the positive in striving to be the best. "I don't think anyone should be criticized for being a perfectionist," she said. "I think it's a great trait. . . . The more perfect you can be, the better."[5]

In the meantime, Stewart's merchandise began to come out. The Martha Stewart Wedding Invitation Collection was released, and other products weren't far behind. No longer was Stewart just a single person who wrote a few books; she was quickly building a larger brand. Products stamped with Stewart's name on them sold well because of her signature. Her followers seemed to trust Stewart's advice, expecting the same perfection in her products as they found in her recipes and craft projects.

As Stewart's base of fans grew, even psychologists weighed in on her popularity. They debated whether women were feeling guilty because they felt as if they were neglecting their homes and families as they focused more on their careers. In the late 1980s, the first generation

WESTPORT, CONNECTICUT

Martha Stewart was not the only famous person to have lived in Westport, Connecticut. The town of more than 25,000 people, less than an hour from New York City, has long been known as a hangout for celebrities.

That image dates to the early 1900s when writers, artists, actors, musicians, and other creative types discovered the place along the Saugatuck River, which leads to the Long Island Sound. F. Scott Fitzgerald was living there when he wrote part of his American classic, *The Great Gatsby*, which was published in 1925. Other famous people who live (or lived) there include actresses Elizabeth Taylor, Tallulah Bankhead, and Bette Davis, aviation hero Charles Lindbergh, writer Rod Serling of *The Twilight Zone*, singer Michael Bolton, songwriter Neil Sedaka, and former TV talk-show host Phil Donahue and his wife, Marlo Thomas.

Perhaps the most famous couple, though, was Paul Newman and his wife, Joanne Woodward. Newman, who died in September 2008, was one of the biggest movie stars of his time, starring in such major films as *Cool Hand Luke*, *Butch Cassidy and the Sundance Kid*, and *The Sting*. He was nominated nine times for an Academy Award, winning an Oscar in 1986 for *The Color of Money*. In addition, Newman was a race-car driver and was the co-owner of a racing team. He also started Newman's Own, which produces a range of food products, from salad of women who were set on having careers were well into adulthood and some were actively enjoying more fulfilling lives in the working world. Other experts spoke for a different type of woman. They said that those who had less stimulating, low-paying jobs read Stewart's books because

dressings to salsas; it has donated more than $200 million to charitable causes. And he ran a camp for seriously ill children in Connecticut. Woodward has been nominated for four Academy Awards, winning one in 1958 for her role in *The Three Faces of Eve*. She and Newman starred in several movies together. Woodward now runs the prestigious Westport Country Playhouse, which stages numerous plays.

Many films and TV shows have been filmed or set in Westport, including the movie *The Stepford Wives* and the television series *I Love Lucy*.

The town's reputation as a home to the rich and famous is a far cry from its roots. Westport was founded in the mid-1600s. During the Revolutionary War, British troops landed at nearby Compo Beach and fought the local militia before setting some buildings in the area ablaze. Today, a statue at Compo Beach commemorates the fight, and the local cemetery houses the graves of the men who died in the battle.

It wasn't until 1835, behind the efforts of a leading citizen, Daniel Nash, that the location was incorporated as Westport. It was a successful farming community during the 1800s, known for growing onions. Today, it is one of the most affluent communities in the United States, with most homes selling for more than $2 million.

the articles and recipes infused readers with an excitement about entertaining, whether or not they used the information. Apparently, these women were having vicarious social experiences just by reading Stewart's books. Nonetheless, millions of women across America were opening Martha Stewart books and changing the way they thought about their meals and their homes.

MARTHA ON THE NEWSSTAND

About this time, Stewart began to contemplate starting a magazine. It was 1990 when she and 37 other people gathered in New York to develop a preview issue for such a publication. Stewart had a dream—the magazine would concentrate on domesticity, the topic that had been her focus as she produced book after book and event after event. It was not long before the magazine project was well under way.

It had been decided that the magazine would be called *Martha Stewart Living*, after its founder, and that the first issue would be published in December 1990. The staff was busy. While Stewart traveled across the country that summer giving lectures about entertaining and selling her books in cities such as Detroit, St. Louis, and Seattle, she and her staff also prepared articles and photographs to be used in the premiere issue of the magazine.[6] Stewart always seemed to be working on more than one job at a time.

Most of the pictures in the first issue of *Martha Stewart Living* were taken at Turkey Hill, or in areas surrounding the home. On a sunny, warm day in August, Stewart wore a wool sweater and hat as she pretended to be shopping for a Christmas tree. A photographer took pictures, as this scene would be part of the magazine. There was a how-to article about designing, building, and decorating a kitchen, based on the elaborate version that Stewart and her husband had built in their home a few years before. Another story

Martha Stewart is shown in a photograph from 1990. Stewart achieved a milestone that year, as she launched the first issue of her magazine, *Martha Stewart Living*, in December. The publication was an immediate success.

featured children as they decorated Christmas cookies. There was also a glossary of Christmas trees, and many holiday cooking and gift-giving ideas.[7] In the end, more than a half-million copies of the magazine rolled off the printing presses. A new Martha Stewart product had been born, complete with the founder's picture—perched on a porch of her home—on the cover!

"Martha taught us to dream big," magazine editor Susan Wyland told a reporter several years later.[8] With the magazine's release, Stewart's popularity continued to grow. By 1991, she had signed a deal with Time Warner so that she could expand her business. Already, she had produced four entertainment-based videos through the company that was publishing her books, and her television special, *At Home with Martha Stewart This Christmas*, had appeared at Christmas time on the Lifetime channel for two years.[9]

By 1993, the bi-monthly *Martha Stewart Living* was a big success with hundreds of thousands of readers, and Stewart was appearing twice a month on the *Today* show and giving lectures across the country. As if that was not keeping her busy enough, her television show *Martha Stewart Living* debuted in September 1993. The half-hour program was filmed in her Westport kitchen and in the gardens that surrounded the house.[10] It was shown once a week on 110 television stations across the country.

"I'm totally busy," Stewart told a writer from *USA Today* one morning as she traveled from her Westport home to the magazine's offices in New York City. "I just have to be organized, and I have to rely on a lot of help."[11]

On her television show, Stewart offered recipes and decorating tips, gardening advice, wisdom about refinishing furniture and other household chores, and more. Viewers across America seemed to love it. "We're trying to give people ideas that they can really do," Stewart explained. "We want to be a superior how-to program."[12]

MARTHA AND MADONNA

Meanwhile, she continued to develop more products and bolster her brand. Curiously, she looked to the pop star Madonna as an example of a woman who had built a business around her own talent—and her own name. "She identifies with Madonna on a business level," explained entertainment attorney Allen Grubman, who was representing both women in 1995. "She wants to build a business around her creativity, just as Madonna has."[13]

Stewart understood that a multimedia approach to business was coming. She began to post information about upcoming television broadcasts in each issue of her magazine, and the two entities worked in tandem, sometimes even addressing similar subject matter during the same months.

Stewart worked tirelessly with her growing media conglomerate. Still getting by on only three to four hours of sleep a night, she sometimes called friends in the very early morning hours. And she never seemed to be doing one thing at a time—she was always juggling multiple tasks and talents. She once even confessed to a friend that she was cleaning the telephone with Windex while they were talking.[14]

But without all of her passion and energy, Stewart would probably not have become a household name. Certainly, she knew how to lead a growing team of employees who admired her abilities. From the time she opened her catering business and published her first book, *Entertaining*, she had hired several women from her Westport neighborhood who contributed their time and talents to building the business. In the acknowledgments for that first book, Stewart thanked the dozens of participants who helped in the publishing effort—including her husband, her daughter, friends, neighbors, and family.

There was no way that Martha Stewart could have created this business without their help, and she knew that. Meanwhile, many of those who worked for her marveled at the expertise she had in dealing with diverse situations, from making a delicious tart to marketing a television program.

Despite the end of her marriage, Stewart seemed content. She kept several homes for herself now that Alexis lived on her own. Besides Turkey Hill, she spent time at a house in East Hampton, on Long Island, and kept a small apartment in New York. "I'm not an unhappy person," she told a reporter from *The New York Times* in 1994. "I wish people understood me better. I'd like to have my negotiations on all my business things be shorter. Silly things like that. But on the whole, I haven't had many disappointments. I've really been pretty lucky."[15]

Around the same time, this goddess of domesticity decided to purchase another home, an iconic modern house in East Hampton that had been built by the architect Gordon Bunshaft in 1962. The house was made of concrete and had been given to New York City's Museum of Modern Art in the architect's will, so Stewart purchased it from the museum. It was her first experience with a house that featured very modern architecture. She appreciated the home's design, although, of course, she immediately began to plan for some changes. The house wasn't large, and its rather austere interior was a drastic departure from the cozy homes that she had had in the past, such as the small Victorian cottage she also had in East Hampton. Her new home had only a small kitchen, a living room and dining room that were combined, a bedroom, and a small studio.[16] Now, Stewart had one more project to work on and one

Martha Stewart visited the convention of the National Association of Television Program Executives in January 1994 to promote her new syndicated series, *Martha Stewart Living*. In its first years, the program was a weekly half-hour show, shot mainly at her home in Westport, Connecticut.

more home to add to the collection that she seemed to be accumulating.

Through her adult life, Stewart has often been asked who had mentored her. In fact, Stewart's business has evolved through the years, with the knowledge she accumulated as a child growing up in Nutley supplemented by her many travels and interviews with chefs and other experts. She often admired the famed chef Julia Child, who invited Stewart to appear on a television program called *Baking with Julia* in 1995. Years before receiving the invitation, Stewart had made every recipe in Child's book, *Mastering the Art of French Cooking*, as she prepared herself for her catering career.

"I don't know why people are so mean about her," Child once told a reporter for *People Weekly*. "Probably because she's so successful."[17]

Child and Stewart eventually became acquainted, and the two cooking pros agreed to be interviewed by a reporter as they prepared to appear on Child's cooking program at her home near Boston. "I was brought up with good, fresh, homemade food, but many of my friends were eating out of boxes and cans," Stewart told the reporter. "Now, because of the health craze, people want something better. Look at the sushi and fresh pasta crazes. Young people really care what they're eating." The two women talked a bit more about the state of cooking and eating healthy, before they went on to their next project of the day: cooking up a television show that viewers would find delicious.[18]

NO CHEESE AND CRACKERS

As Stewart's fame ballooned, she was invited to appear on other television programs, too. She was a special guest on Ellen DeGeneres's sitcom, *Ellen*, in 1995. Stewart played herself appearing at a book signing at the bookstore owned by DeGeneres's character. A funny moment in the show came when Stewart brought in a basket of fancy snacks. "I always like to have something a little special so that these book signings are a little bit more homey," Stewart said. "Some people just have cheese and crackers," she added, glancing at the cheese and crackers that the show's lead character had provided.[19]

Certainly, Martha Stewart was making an impact across the United States. In 1996, she was named to *Time* magazine's list of 25 Most Influential Americans. Also on the list were comedian and television star Jerry Seinfeld, talk-show host Oprah Winfrey, and architect Frank Gehry. "Martha Stewart's inexhaustible brand of domesticity claims a sizable audience," wrote *Time*'s editors.[20]

As Stewart's popularity grew, so did the number of her detractors. In 1996, a calendar was produced that parodied the magazine with its title, *Is Martha Stewart Living?* Meanwhile, Stewart made television appearances and joked with comedians like David Letterman. Her wry sense of humor is often overlooked but, in fact, she does appreciate good jokes. For example, in Stewart's own Christmas special, Miss Piggy did a skit mocking Stewart's perfectionist ways as the Muppet created a gingerbread house.[21]

But media coverage of Stewart also showed an intriguing side to the workaholic businesswoman. One reporter wrote about spending the entire day trying to call Stewart for interviews at appointed times. "Um, am I catching you at a bad time?" the reporter asked just after Stewart put her on hold to command her staff to begin to clean up. The reporter and Stewart had already had a discussion about why the reporter had not called an hour earlier when Stewart was expecting her. As it turned out, the timing was bad. "Yes," said Stewart. "I have a house full of people. We are shooting the Easter magazine."

The reporter followed up again, calling at the newly appointed time of 3 P.M. only to have the phone answered by various household helpers who told her that Stewart was unavailable. Finally, more than an hour later, the two connected. "What do you want?" Stewart abruptly asked.[22] Thus, the busier Stewart's life became, the more challenging her life became for others involved with it.

Yet, Stewart continued to collect a loyal following of readers and television viewers. Susan Wyland, a one-time editor of *Martha Stewart Living*, told a writer from *Newsweek* that Stewart's fans fell into two categories: the Do-Marthas and the Be-Marthas. The Do-Marthas may follow a recipe or re-cover a chair, but they do not take the tasks all too seriously, Wyland said. The Be-Marthas are the fans who obsess about Stewart's cooking and other home projects in their own efforts to be perfect homemakers.[23]

On her own homefront, Stewart had begun to date others after her divorce, including an art dealer and a media mogul, but it seemed that the independent and successful woman had yet to find another man she would want to marry. Even though she was initially distraught over her divorce, she made fast friends. When Stewart needed to draw a crowd for a photo shoot, or just a simple meal, it was never a problem to attract a few friends.

Her friendships went beyond the dining room table. She went climbing in the Himalayas with a New York socialite and traveled to Poland with a journalist and his wife. "She's no whiner," the socialite, Sandy Hill Pittman, said of Stewart. "If you say, 'Let's go see the sunrise over the Himalayas at 4 A.M.,' and it means walking five vertical miles, she's there."[24]

Building an
Omni-Business

The amazingly efficient Martha Stewart continued to stun and surprise people. As an indication of her growing celebrity status, *People Weekly* listed her in 1996 among the 50 most beautiful people in the world. The image of the tall, radiant woman was seen almost everywhere—from the TV screen to the covers of her books and magazines. Everyone, it seemed, wanted to be like Stewart.

Perhaps, though, not everyone wanted to work as hard as she did. Stewart arose at 5 each morning to do some online business. By 5:30, she started to exercise and was off and running into a busy day. Activity, she said, kept her vibrant.[1]

Sometimes her obligations included events staged by the media. Such was the case when Stewart gathered with two other women at a friend's Manhattan penthouse at the request of *Fortune* magazine. The three women sipped cocktails and talked about careers, success, other women, and men. "Martha is unbelievably curious," said one of the women, Charlotte Beers, chief executive of the advertising firm Ogilvy & Mather. "The greatest knowledge seeker I have ever met."[2] Despite that comment, Stewart confided that she would love to get more education, since her formal schooling had stopped years ago after her graduation from Barnard. In reality, though, Stewart had never stopped learning. Whether it was building a shed or starting a new magazine, Stewart has always made sure she learned new tasks.

MULTIMEDIA WINDFALL

By the mid-1990s, *Martha Stewart Living* magazine had a circulation of 1.3 million, and it was named the Magazine of the Year in 1996 by *AdWeek*, the advertising trade publication. About five million people were watching her syndicated half-hour television program, and she packed additional television specials into her already-busy schedule, like the hourlong *Home for Holidays* show. Stewart's show had received several Daytime Emmy Awards, and it was being dubbed in various languages so that it could be seen in other countries—like Japan, Portugal, Brazil, and Germany.[3]

In addition, five million copies of her 14 books had been sold, she had produced six videos, and her lines of sheets, towels, and paints were marketed by various retailers.

The success of her TV show and magazine led Stewart to renegotiate her relationship with Time Inc., which financed the two entities. Stewart persuaded Time to create a subsidiary called Martha Stewart Living Enterprises and to name Stewart as its chief executive officer. Time provided the funds for the company, and Stewart provided the ideas and her name. The new subsidiary encompassed the magazine and its spinoff books, the television show, and Stewart's *Today* show appearances. Her royalties from Kmart and the books she had written from 1982 to 1995 were not included.

TAKING CONTROL

By 1997, Martha Stewart Living Enterprises had annual revenues of $200 million because of all of the work its creator had done with the help of her ever-growing staff. Stewart realized that it was time to really become her own boss, as she decided to purchase the company from Time.[4] Stewart arranged the purchase of at least 80 percent of the company for $75 million, although accounts vary. Time's remaining stake was estimated at between 5 and 10 percent. With the purchase, Stewart renamed the company Martha Stewart Living Omnimedia.

By now, the company included not only her magazines, books, and television shows, but also a Web site at www.marthastewart.com and a syndicated newspaper column that was distributed by *The New York Times*. In addition, she developed a mail-order catalog that included some of her inspiring projects. Despite warnings from business

DID YOU KNOW?

When Martha Stewart Living Omnimedia was formed, the new company developed an organizational chart that was typically Martha—a family tree. Each manager on the chart was represented by a tree. Stewart was a beech tree, and, according to *The New York Times*, the accompanying description said, "The beech tree, also referred to as the mother tree, is one of the most beautiful and popular of the large shade trees."

Martha Stewart examined the packaging and display of her line of household accessories during a June 1997 visit to a Kmart store. That same year, she created a new company, Martha Stewart Living Omnimedia, after purchasing it from Time Inc.

critics, Stewart even entered a new, major partnership agreement with Kmart that would place "Martha Stewart Everyday" boutiques, featuring her low-priced linens, paints, and videos, in each of Kmart's 2,145 stores.[5] Indeed, Stewart seemed to have a keen business mind that had no limitations.

She was always thinking of new ideas, whether for her business or for her fans. "Here's one way to make your mark," she wrote in her 1997 book *Good Things*. "Emboss initials onto plain paper napkins when you're entertaining a crowd."[6] She told her readers where they could buy an embosser and how to create one so that they could mono-gram other belongings. Indeed, part of Stewart's genius was in developing ideas no one had thought of before. While other people might have just gone out and bought cloth napkins, Stewart presented her readers with an idea that few party-goers would have ever seen. "It's a good thing," was a trademark saying that she had used for years—in her magazine and books and on her television programs.

THE CRITICS WEIGH IN

Despite all of her successes, her critics still fussed. Some observers simply did not like her personality, but oth-ers expressed concerns about her business acumen. They thought that her company was growing too fast, and they were not keen on her partnership with Kmart.

"I don't think the Martha Stewart brand is as strong as it was a year ago," one consultant ventured in 1998. He, among others, talked about the possibility that the one-time caterer from Westport was spreading herself too thin with her many business entities. Stewart, the consultant added, "has endorsed a lot of areas that don't equate to one cogent brand, from inexpensive, low-end retail, to TV programs where she's attempting to pitch to a very different audience."[7]

Certainly, there were advertisers who believed in the Martha Stewart brand, and they did not seem to be shying away from buying ads in her magazine or on her television show. The Ford Motor Company, in 1998, committed to spend $10 million with Martha Stewart Living Omnimedia. Ford's Mercury division would sponsor the Cookie of the Week segment on Stewart's television show—the company seemed to know that many of its potential customers were fans of Martha Stewart.[8]

Stewart continued to look for other business partnerships. She became a regular guest on CBS's *This Morning*, traveling to Cuba to cover a visit by the Pope and then flying to Japan to cover the Olympics. In addition, in the fall of 1997, her television show *Martha Stewart Living* went from being broadcast one day a week to six days a week, creating a greater need for more ideas and themes. "I'll be on every show," Stewart emphatically told a reporter. "It may not be me rolling out the pastries all the time, but it will be my show and I'll be hosting it."[9] In 1998, *Martha*

IN HER OWN WORDS

Martha Stewart believes that companies have to be aware of their impact on the world that surrounds them and should explore ways of making eco-friendly practices a part of their business plans. In the September 2007 issue of *Martha Stewart Living*, she wrote:

> It is impossible to celebrate the value of healthy living without considering the health of the environment in which we live.

Stewart Living achieved first place among daily syndicated series, according to Nielsen Syndicated Service.

By this point, Stewart had several working kitchens from which she filmed her shows—one at her longtime home at Turkey Hill in Westport and another in East Hampton. Stewart spent $4 million on a third kitchen studio, also located in Westport, to make it more suitable for taping television and radio programs. The new facility included a beautiful kitchen where her staff could eat catered lunches and a work-out facility where they could exercise. At this point, Stewart had 230 employees and she had hired the former financial administrator of the New York Yankees to oversee her business.[10] Indeed, Martha Stewart the mega-caterer had grown into a mega-businesswoman.

Stewart had started to tape a 90-second radio spot called "Ask Martha," which was a spin-off of her newspaper column, and by November 1998, she had produced her twenty-second book, *Martha Stewart's Healthy Quick Cook*. It seemed that the queen of domesticity never ran out of ideas. The more she accomplished, the more ideas she produced.

In another book that came out the same year, *Decorating for the Holidays*, Stewart and her staff created a whole chapter about building snowmen. "Like clay or cookie dough, snow practically demands to be shaped," she wrote. "Who can resist?" Snow sculptures included a dog and a little girl decorating an evergreen tree. The girl wore tinsel on her head, around her neck, and along the bottom of a snowy skirt, while the dog wore a collar of tinfoil.[11] The book also offered multiple decorating and gift ideas. Only a few recipes, such as those for gingerbread cookies and icing, were included.

Around the same time, Stewart's paint colors were introduced. Among the colors were those inspired by the

In April 1998, Martha Stewart showed off one of the kitchen studios in her new television production facility in Westport, Connecticut. Stewart spent $4 million to build the facility.

soft tones of the egg shells from her Araucana chickens. Besides Kmart, Sears also started to sell her paints.[12]

As critics worried about the company's quick growth, predicting doom and gloom for the fast-growing business, the queen of the kitchen seemed very content. Each Monday, fresh flowers that were coordinated with her magazine's cover were delivered to the magazine's offices. At her Westport home, she now kept company with four dogs and six cats. She modeled her career after successful businessmen like retailer Ralph Lauren and Microsoft's Bill Gates. Stewart herself seemed sure that her namesake business would survive even if she were no longer able to lead it. Others who watched the market knew she was successful. "The people who follow Martha are cult-like," said one expert in marketing, "which, if you're a marketer—as Martha would say—is a very good thing."[13]

A Powerful Force

Martha Stewart's fans were fiercely loyal, and they looked to her trustworthy leadership, whatever the occasion. Amazingly, Stewart's entire empire—now worth tens of millions of dollars—was built on the basics of cooking, gardening, and homemaking that she learned as a child growing up in Nutley, New Jersey. "Mother and I started baking fruitcakes and cookies and making mincemeat early in the month, and we didn't stop cracking nuts, sifting flour, and preserving fruits until we were absolutely sure that every one of our family's friends and relatives had a wonderful homemade gift.,"[1] she wrote in another holiday book, *Christmas with Martha Stewart Living*.

Certainly, Stewart's early lessons had paid off well and her celebrity status seemed firmly in place. In June 1999, she was invited to the White House for a state dinner in honor of the president of Hungary. But Stewart's outfit for the dinner caused a stir—she selected a seasonably pink ensemble created by Ralph Lauren that featured capri slacks. "I admire Martha Stewart tremendously," a former White House social secretary said. "But I think she needs to read other people's books on how to dress properly for such an occasion. A state dinner means a long dress to the floor."[2]

Stewart's opinion, however, differed. How dare a social secretary give the former model advice on how to dress? "Martha felt it was appropriate," Stewart's spokeswoman responded, "and she said a number of people complimented her on it."[3]

GOING PUBLIC

That year, 1999, was important for other reasons, too. For Stewart's business, there was a big change. She went from being the sole owner in her company to being just one of many owners. Martha Stewart Living Omnimedia went public—meaning that people could be part-owners of the company by purchasing shares of stock. For the first time ever, on October 19, 1999, Martha Stewart Living Omnimedia was offered for sale on the New York Stock Exchange.

Stewart and her business associates traveled to cities throughout the United States and Europe, rallying interest among those who might have wanted to own a piece of her growing multimedia company. "The mood was festive, the business community receptive," Stewart reported in her magazine in December of that year.[4] Even though she was already a very important businesswoman, launching her company into the public realm would have interesting implications in Stewart's future. For now, though, the stock

Martha Stewart attended a state dinner at the White House in June 1999 during the official visit of the president of Hungary. Some etiquette experts criticized Stewart for wearing this light-pink pantsuit, saying that the occasion required more formal attire.

price quickly rose, increasing the value of Stewart's share in her company from its original estimates of $250 million to $1.06 billion by the time the initial public offering was finished. Now, that's not a bad day at the office![5]

Indeed, even the people who had become known for making fun of Stewart, such as one of the authors of the *Is Martha Stewart Living?* parody, stopped joking about her. "She's less ridiculous," writer James Downey explained. "She's a serious corporate chieftain."[6] It seemed as though Stewart had gained new respect from people who had watched her develop her business from the ground up.

By this time, Stewart had produced 27 books that had sold 9.5 million copies. She now had two magazines—*Martha Stewart Living* and *Martha Stewart Weddings*—read by an estimated 10 million people each month, and her television show continued, while she also hosted specials for the holidays. In 1998 and 1999, *Forbes* named her among the 50 Most Powerful Women. She was appearing weekly with Bryant Gumbel on *The Early Show* on CBS and, by then, her retail products were reportedly earning more than $700 million a year.[7] No one seemed surprised at her success, or the ideas she created—she once even built a giant pyramid cake made of Rice Krispies squares for the Kmart chairman.[8] Martha Stewart Living Omnimedia now had a staff of more than 400 people, and the company's founder began to delegate more responsibilities to them.

By the time Stewart's company went public, the home-making maven had collected a fair number of homes, too. She now owned the two houses in East Hampton; two in Westport, Connecticut; another in Seal Harbor, Maine; and a Manhattan penthouse, where she rarely stayed.[9] Meanwhile, Stewart had been rumored to have various companions—from a wealthy software mogul to a British actor. Even though she periodically expressed a desire to remarry, she had not done so.

Despite her busy days at the office, Stewart began to contemplate moving away from her beloved home at Turkey Hill, even writing an essay for *The New York Times* about how much Westport had changed and grown since she and Andy had initially purchased their house. Stewart found a new homestead in Bedford, New York—a large 152-acre estate called Cantitoe Corners, which she purchased for about $15.2 million. Cantitoe Corners included five homes—the oldest was a historic 1784 farmhouse; also on the estate were an 1897 cottage, a 1929 "winter house," and two additional houses that were built in 1969.[10]

Certainly, there would be much work to get done now at Bedford, even though it would be years before Stewart would actually move in.

A HOUSEHOLD NAME

Martha Kostyra Stewart was now extremely wealthy. Her name was known by nearly everyone in the United States.

NEW YORK STOCK EXCHANGE

The New York Stock Exchange (NYSE) can be found on one of the most famous streets in the world: Wall Street in New York City. The NYSE is the oldest stock exchange in America. It was founded in 1792.

What is a stock exchange? It is a collection of companies that people can buy stock in. (Other stock exchanges include the American Stock Exchange and Nasdaq, and other countries also have stock exchanges.)

Some of the companies listed on the NYSE include Martha Stewart Living Omnimedia, Wal-Mart, and the Coca-Cola Company. On the NYSE, each company has a symbol instead of using its name. (Martha Stewart Living Omnimedia is MSO, Wal-Mart is WMT, and Coca-Cola is KO).

Companies listed on the New York Stock Exchange are also called public companies. Unlike private ones, people can own a piece of public companies by buying shares of stock. A share is what it will cost to own that piece. For example, one share of a company listed on the New York Stock Exchange could cost $19. Once you buy a company's shares of stock, you can attend the company's annual meeting and vote on issues. In short, you have a say in how the company is run. The more shares you own, the more input you have. Martha Stewart owns a bulk of

She had helped decorate the White House Christmas tree, and she was much loved by many people across the country. At home, she had the good company of her dogs, seven fluffy Himalayan cats, and a few birds. She had collected the cats from the same breeder and called them Teeny, Weeny, Mozart, Verdi, Vivaldi, Bartok, and Berlioz. "They are friendly and affectionate but not demanding;

shares in Martha Stewart Living Omnimedia, so she has a large impact on company decisions.

In private companies, the owners do not have to share any information about their business with anyone. Public companies, however, are required by law to disclose all kinds of information, including how much money the business makes or loses each year and the salaries of top executives.

The most important reason people buy shares of stock is to make money. These shareholders put their cash into a company thinking that over time its value will increase. For example, if you buy a share for $19, two years from now that share may be worth $38. If you sell your stock at that point, you earned a profit of $19, which means you doubled your money.

Companies sell shares so they can raise more money to try to improve the business. That is why Stewart decided that her company should be listed on the New York Stock Exchange. When shares of Martha Stewart Living Omnimedia went up for sale, Martha Stewart became a billionaire overnight. The stock sold at $18 when her company went public in October 1999; two days later, it was selling for $40 a share. When a company is first listed with a stock exchange, it is called an initial public offering (IPO).

At the New York Stock Exchange, Martha Stewart rang the opening bell on October 19, 1999—the day her company, Martha Stewart Living Omnimedia, went public. Standing with her were William Johnston, the president of the New York Stock Exchange, and Sharon Patrick, the president and chief operating officer of Martha Stewart Living Omnimedia.

they are quiet and easy to care for; and they get along well with people and other animals," she once wrote in the "Ask Martha" section of her magazine. Because of Stewart's popularity, the article prompted the New York-based breeder to be flooded with hundreds of phone calls asking for kittens. Apparently, many fans even trusted Stewart when it came to the kinds of pets they should have. "I have to turn most people away," the breeder told a reporter for *The New York Times*.[11]

Still, it seemed that either people loved Stewart or they were put off by her perfectionist habits and rather cool personality. As Stewart's life had grown busier and her success had ballooned, she had even less patience than she did earlier in her career. "If Stewart has a flaw in her role as the hostess of the great American dinner party, it is in fact that she comes off being a bit chilly," said a writer for the online site *Slate* in the summer of 2001.[12]

Yet, Stewart was undaunted when it came to her expanding business empire. In early 2001, she announced that the *Martha Stewart Baby* magazine, which had previously published two issues a year, would expand to four issues a year. "Our monthly magazine, *Martha Stewart Living* has become synonymous with trusted content for the homemaker," Stewart wrote in a media release about the baby publication. "Our quarterly magazine, *Martha Stewart Weddings*, provides the bride-to-be with impeccable information and inspiration. With *Martha Stewart Baby*, we now reach another demographic, those readers who need a different kind of content that will help make the nurturing, raising, and education of young children a meaningful and fulfilling occupation."[13]

UNCERTAIN TIMES

Then, the terrorist attacks of September 11, 2001, occurred, as two airplanes crashed into the World Trade Center in New York City. And, like all New York-based businesses, the Martha Stewart empire felt the effects. The *Martha Stewart Living* magazine experienced a dip in its revenues as fewer advertisers purchased magazine space. That was similar to what was happening at most publications across the country. Yet, the turmoil and economic downturn of the time did not dissuade Stewart and her advisors from expanding their business. She began to talk of selling furniture and floor coverings, as well, under the Martha Stewart Signature label.[14] And she announced plans to expand geographically, bringing her magazines, TV shows, and merchandising into Western Europe.

Perhaps it was the uncertainty of the economic times and the unease felt after the terrorist attacks, but Martha Stewart seemed to become even more popular. "What Martha is selling is the idea that domestic perfection

BEDFORD, NEW YORK

Bedford, New York, where Martha Stewart purchased an estate in 1999, is 48 miles (77 kilometers) north of New York City with a population of more than 18,000 people. It is in Westchester County, one of the most affluent counties in the nation.

The town was founded in 1680 when New England Puritans from Stamford, Connecticut, bought three square miles of land from Chief Katonah and other Indians. The Puritans first built a meetinghouse, a gristmill on the Mianus River, and a cemetery. At first, Bedford was in Connecticut, but King William III of England ruled in 1700—before the colonies became the United States—that the town belonged to New York.

During part of the Revolutionary War, Bedford served as the county seat. Although burned by the British on July 11, 1779, the town recovered, and after the battle, it was the main home of county government until replaced by White Plains.

Bedford consists of three hamlets: Bedford Village, Katonah, and Bedford Hills. Bedford Village is the original settlement and features the Village Green and historic buildings, including a courthouse built in 1787 that now houses a museum. Katonah is known for its Victorian architecture. It is also home to the Caramoor Center for Music and the Arts (a restored residence is possible," wrote *Newsweek* design writer Cathleen McGuigan in 2002. "That's a big, whopping fantasy, but it's fun."[15] In her article, McGuigan defended Stewart against claims in a recent book that slammed her alleged selfish practices. "She's an impossibly bright-eyed, consistent woman, magically competent, who has far more than 24

that has outdoor theaters) and the 62-acre John Jay Homestead, which has 12 structures, including the retirement home of John Jay, the first chief justice of the United State Supreme Court. Bedford Hills includes the business district, town government, and the police department. It is the site of the state's largest women's prison, the Bedford Hills Correctional Facility. The hamlet was once known as Bedford Station after the railroad was built in 1847. It also has farms and estates.

After many years as a farming community, Bedford began to grow. People were attracted to it not only because of its rural character but also because of its proximity to New York City. Bedford became primarily a suburban, residential town. But it has tried to maintain its roots, taking care of its many streams, ponds, and woods as well as its historic districts. People either live in the historic districts or the rural areas, where there are horse farms or the remnants of old dairy properties. The town has more than 100 miles (161 kilometers) of trails for horseback riding.

A huge white oak, which is believed to be more than 500 years old, stands as an important symbol for the town. In 1977, when development threatened the oak, residents raised money to buy the property to protect it.

hours in her day, to do beautifully all those domestic things that career women can't begin to think about," McGuigan continued.[16]

It wasn't long, however, before the economic downturn affected Stewart's stalwart partner, Kmart. The massive discount company—second only to Wal-Mart in size—filed for bankruptcy protection in early 2002 and had to reorganize its business. Soon, other retailers were trying to lure Stewart to sell her products in their stores instead. They were sure that she would leave the beleaguered Kmart chain, where her products had generated about a $1 billion in sales. Instead, though, Stewart continued to work with Kmart through these difficult times, providing the store with a variety of items from linens to garden tools to kitchenware and decorative items.[17]

As Stewart watched Kmart fight through its challenging financial situation, she was troubled by the ongoing inquiries about her partnership with the company. "Yes, I know the numbers!" she told a writer for *Fortune* magazine early in 2002. "When I signed up as their lifestyle consultant, all I knew was that this was the largest mass merchant in America, and I could reach an audience that was unheard-of for a cookbook author."[18]

However, it had been 15 years since Stewart had begun her relationship with Kmart. Now, other chains, like Wal-Mart, were taking center stage and becoming stronger retail outlets. As an avid reader who followed current events and trends, Stewart was well aware of what was happening in the business world. And it would not be long before she, too, needed a dependable partner in Kmart to help see her through some troubling times. Martha Stewart had lived a fulfilling life with much success, but within a few months, Stewart's own integrity would be questioned.

A Different
Kind of Home

In early 2002, Martha Stewart became the target of an investigation by the Federal Bureau of Investigation, the U.S. Department of Justice, and the U.S. Securities and Exchange Commission. The agencies said that Stewart might have used insider information to make money when she sold stocks that she owned in a biotechnology company called ImClone.

Just a few months earlier, on December 27, 2001, Stewart had sold her ImClone stock just before the company's stock prices took a dramatic decline. She was traveling to a vacation in Mexico with a good friend when she called her broker's assistant and instructed him to sell. That action would cause many questions to be asked over the next several months. Investigators thought that Stewart might have had some inside knowledge about the company, and that could be why she sold the stock before the price started to decline.

This accusation was a stunning blow to the keen businesswoman who had built a billion-dollar enterprise. People around the country started to pay close attention as Stewart's name appeared in the news. Viewers watched the television reports and read newspaper and magazine articles about the ordeal. How did Martha Stewart get into this situation?

"This will all be resolved in the very near future, and I will be exonerated of any ridiculousness," Stewart told an interviewer on CBS's *The Early Show* during her weekly cooking segment in June 2002.[1] While she chopped cabbage in the studio kitchen to create yet another delicious recipe, Stewart tried to portray the importance of good style and good food, while still giving the appearance that all things were in good order. As the interviewer, Jane Clayson, continued to press her about the investigation, Stewart cut her short and said she wanted to focus on making her salad.

All apparently was not perfect, though. Stewart would be the center of the investigation for many more months.

BEHIND IMCLONE

ImClone was a scientific company that had created a treatment for cancer called Erbitux. The company's founder, Sam Waksal, was an immunologist and a businessman who was comfortable among New York's most elite circles. He had become a friend of Stewart's and had at one time even dated Alexis. ImClone's profitability was challenged when the Food and Drug Administration (FDA) would not approve Erbitux for sale, saying sufficient testing was not yet completed. Waksal knew that this would be bad news for his company, so he quickly tried to sell $5 million of his ImClone stock before the news was made public.

On CBS's *The Early Show* in June 2002, Martha Stewart cut cabbage for a salad while anchor Jane Clayson asked her about the investigation into her sale of ImClone stock. By September, Stewart was no longer doing her cooking segments on *The Early Show* because she refused to answer questions about the probe.

Authorities started to ask, too, if Stewart knew the news about the FDA's decision before other people knew it. This was because Stewart sold $228,000 of her own ImClone stock the day before the Erbitux news was reported by the media. Stewart, however, said that she sold her stock because its value on the New York Stock Exchange had fallen below $60; her broker had orders, she said, to sell the stock if it had reached that point.[2] She claimed to have no advance knowledge about the FDA's decision.

Still, by June 2002, her name was all over the newspapers and magazines regarding the poorly timed stock sale.

Everyone wanted to know if Stewart had broken the laws about trading stocks. In the meantime, the bankruptcy of Kmart, which was closing hundreds of its stores, led many people to believe that Stewart's name would soon be worth nothing. "In her well-mannered world, image is everything," a reporter for *Newsweek* wrote. "And even if her ImClone-stock sale was legit—as she insists—the perception of dirty dealing could finally tarnish Martha's Midas touch."[3]

Meanwhile, Martha Stewart Living Omnimedia began to feel the heat as its founder was under fire and a congressional investigation was announced. Stock prices in the company that had gone public just a few years earlier began to fall, which meant that many people who had purchased stock were now losing money.

At the time that Stewart was chopping vegetables for a salad on *The Early Show*, the investigation into her stock sales had begun to examine whether she had orchestrated a cover-up. Congressional investigators wondered if Stewart made false statements to the panel investigating ImClone.[4] By September, Stewart stopped appearing on *The Early Show* because she refused to answer any more questions about the ordeal while she was cooking on the program.[5]

As the messy situation evolved, Stewart kept working. Her own television show continued to air, and her magazine continued to be published. She kept her mind off of her troubles by thinking up creative and unique ideas for the home and for entertaining. Still, her company's value suffered. The price of stock in Martha Stewart Living Omnimedia lost more than 50 percent in value. At one point during the summer, it was estimated that Stewart had lost $235 million of her own wealth because stock prices for Martha Stewart Living Omnimedia had dropped so much. "Her brand identity is about perfection," one advertising executive said. "If what she's accused of is true, it demonstrates a potential flaw."[6]

THE FANS' SUPPORT

Yet, many of Stewarts' fans were in disbelief. They did not think that their idol had done any wrong. One man even started a Web site called SaveMartha.com on which he posted news articles and fans gathered to talk and complain about the investigation. There was much discussion about whether Stewart was being wrongly investigated partly because she was a very successful woman. "Let's face it: Martha, the accused, can't catch a break," Gloria Borger wrote in *U.S. News & World Report*. "Not only is she a high-profile woman; she's also an easy target as an insider who broke into the boys club of finance. Now she's being punished for her temerity."[7]

But by early September, Martha Stewart Living Omnimedia started to look for someone to replace its founder as the chief executive officer. In a headline, *The New York Times* asked: "Is There Life for Martha Stewart Living Omnimedia Without Martha?"[8] Stock prices had fallen from a high of $39.75 a share in 1999 to less than $10 a share. That meant that not only was Stewart losing more money, so were all of the investors in her company.[9]

People began to wonder what would happen next. In July, Stewart skipped an East Hampton fundraiser at which she was being honored. At the annual Hampton Classic horse show in August, local residents were not surprised when Stewart—who had attended for many years—did not show up. Stewart, instead, spent much of the summer focused on her work, talking with her lawyers and keeping as low a profile as she possibly could with her name in the headlines every day.

Quietly, she attended a Native American festival in Maine, where she reportedly paid $400 for a basket. Much of her energy, too, was consumed with the construction of a new, larger house on the Bedford property—a project that was estimated to cost $14.5 million.[10] Meanwhile, Stewart found solace in early morning walks on the beach with her two dogs when she was in Westport.[11]

As September arrived, Stewart resumed filming her television show, but in October she gave a speech to her employees during a break one day. As she thanked them for sticking with her throughout the investigation, she continued to focus on a project, stapling new upholstery onto a cushion. It seemed as though Stewart never stopped for a minute—even when she was addressing something as important as this investigation.[12]

Readers of *Martha Stewart Living* started to notice that photos of Stewart were disappearing from its pages. Pictures of the founder had continuously been on the magazine's cover and throughout its pages. Now, under the scrutiny of a very public scandal, Stewart seemed to be scarce. In the Thanksgiving issue of 2002, a photograph of her rolling pin collection replaced the image of Stewart that usually appeared with her column.[13]

By December, Stewart called off her annual CBS holiday special. Talk-show hosts, comedians, and *Saturday Night Live* made comical references to the now-deflated business-woman. Many people, it seemed, took pleasure in Stewart's tough situation. A book entitled *Martha, Inc.*, became a best seller with its sharp look at her business dealings. And an NBC movie by the same name followed.

All of this turmoil added to Stewart's distress. In June 2003, Martha Stewart Living Omnimedia announced that it expected its founder to be indicted in federal court. This meant that investigators thought they had evidence against Stewart. Her company's stock prices immediately began to fall again.

Now, reports were rampant that the Martha Stewart brand would not survive. Almost like obituaries, news reports of the time assumed that Stewart—and her brand—were gone. "She made the world of style approachable," said one former magazine editor, who spoke in the past tense when she was interviewed by *The New York Times*. "She took us away from those hideous mauves and jades and gave us a clean, logical, sophisticated, and cheerful world."[14]

CHARGED

On June 4, 2003, Stewart was composed and focused. She was dressed in a gray pantsuit and a cream-colored raincoat, as she carried an umbrella with her into the Manhattan courthouse where she was indicted on criminal charges of securities fraud, obstruction of justice, and conspiracy. Stewart was not indicted for improper stock sales, yet the charges against her were still very serious. It was possible that Stewart could go to jail.

In the back of the courtroom, Stewart's daughter, Alexis, waited on a bench.[15] She, too, seemed to find it hard to believe that her hard-working mother could be in such trouble. The case of *The United States vs. Martha Stewart* had begun,[16] and it would be many more months before it would end.

Meanwhile, always the stalwart businesswoman, Stewart had been thinking ahead. She had hired a crisis management firm to help her company soften the damage that would occur if she were indicted. Within hours of the indictment, factual details of the case were posted on a Web site called marthatalks.com—all part of a grand plan to keep Stewart's fans informed about the case against her. Immediately, the site began to receive millions of hits.[17]

The next day, Stewart stepped down as chairman and chief executive officer of the company that she had grown. This was considered the most appropriate action that she could take at the time. In her place, two people were chosen. A company director by the name of Jeff Ubben became the new chairman. And Sharon Patrick, a former consultant whom Stewart had met 10 years earlier when climbing

Martha Stewart is shown leaving the federal courthouse in Manhattan on June 4, 2003. She was indicted on charges of securities fraud, obstruction of justice, and conspiracy. After her indictment, Stewart vowed to fight the charges.

Mount Kilimanjaro in Africa, became CEO. Patrick had been the company's president since 1997.[18]

After her indictment, Stewart promised that she would fight the charges. If she was found guilty, she could face up to 30 years in prison and $2 million in fines. Now there was even more discussion about the amount of publicity the case was getting. Some people said that prosecutors were using her to demonstrate that they were coming down hard on cases involving stock-market fraud. Others were still convinced that Stewart's case was rooted in the fact that she was a woman. "Her gender plays some part in this," said Lou Dobbs, a male CNN anchor. "We wouldn't hear the criticism that I've heard of her aggressive defense if she were a male CEO."[19]

Despite the indictment in June, Stewart tried to live as normally as possible. She spent much time with her elderly mother, Martha Kostyra, and her 37-year-old daughter. And that summer she started to attend the various charity benefits and garden fairs around her Westport and East Hampton homes. One Sunday, she went to a favorite restaurant on the Upper East Side of Manhattan. "She seems to be in better spirits since the indictment. At least now it's not hanging like a sword of Damocles over her head," the friend she dined with told a reporter for *People Weekly*.[20]

By October, it seemed, Stewart's demeanor was changing. Despite the financial losses her situation was causing her, as well as a decrease in ad sales for her magazine, she seemed to be more relaxed. She became less intense with the people who worked around her as she traveled to Italy, went to parties, and had business dinners. A few weeks later, in November, Stewart appeared in an interview with Barbara Walters as they toured her hometown of Nutley, New Jersey. "Of course I'm scared," she said when asked about the potential jail sentence. "I don't think I'll be going to jail."[21]

THE TRIAL BEGINS

As her trial finally started in early February 2004, Stewart appeared calm. Wearing a trademark pantsuit and carrying an expensive handbag, she entered the courtroom apparently ready to get the long-awaited trial under way.[22] Alexis attended the trial to support her mother nearly every day. "You couldn't have kept me away," she said in a later interview with Larry King.[23]

Around the country, there was much interest in Stewart's trial from both her fans and her detractors. Even actress Rosie O'Donnell showed up at the courthouse one day with M&Ms for Stewart, offering her support. The days were long and the testimony was sometimes intense as prosecutors tried to prove that Stewart had broken the law. Stewart, meanwhile, persevered even though she lost at least one long-time friend, when the woman with whom she often traveled abroad testified against her. In the midst of the trial, Kmart filed a lawsuit against Martha Stewart Living Omnimedia, saying that it overcharged the financially distraught retailer for the exclusive rights to sell Martha Stewart products. It seemed that Stewart's world was caving in on her.

As her trial continued, though, her businesses stayed focused. Stewart had good employees in the appropriate positions, and her company's four divisions continued to make a profit. Her publications, including not only *Martha Stewart Living* but *Martha Stewart Weddings*, *Martha Stewart Kids*, and *Martha Stewart Baby*, were valued at an estimated $182.6 million. In addition, her syndicated television show, *Martha Stewart Living*, and other programming were estimated at $26.69 million. Her merchandising division, offering products through Kmart and other companies, had an estimated value of $48.9 million. And her Internet division, featuring catalog sales, marthastewart.com and marthaflowers.com, was valued at $36.87 million.[24] In all, despite her legal woes, Stewart continued to be a very wealthy woman, with her company's value estimated at more than $295 million.

Success, though, did not transfer to the courtroom. In early March, Martha Stewart was found guilty of the charges against her. When the verdict was read, Stewart appeared stunned. Alexis and one of Stewart's attorneys cried in the courtroom, and Alexis later said that she fainted.[25] Soon after, Stewart went to a private room in the courthouse and called her mother. The billionaire homemaker had bad news to share, yet she seemed to be one of the calmest people in the room.

In the days that followed, Stewart's mother, Alexis, a brother, and a sister gathered at Turkey Hill to commiserate with one another and to offer Stewart some support.

Family and friends kept her company throughout the following days as she contemplated what the future might bring. On the Sunday morning after the verdict, Stewart worked out on her treadmill and discussed gardens while she hiked with an old friend. Even though the verdict saddened her, Stewart could not stop herself from offering solutions for gardening challenges. "She was definitely subdued," the friend said. "She asked me about my garden. She thought I should have a trellis with euonymus, an evergreen bush."[26]

BEFORE HER SENTENCING

It would be months before Stewart knew how long her jail sentence would be and whether she would have to pay a fine. Partly, Stewart was saddened by the great numbers of people who seemed to take glee from her conviction. And she was surprised that so many people apparently disliked her, despite her amazing successes.

The week after the verdict, several television stations took previously taped episodes of *Martha Stewart Living* off the air. An unscientific poll on *People*'s Web site found that respondents were split—half of the people thought that Stewart should go to jail and the other half thought that she should not. Newspapers and magazines carried articles about Stewart's going to prison, many suggesting that she would be put in a minimum-security prison in Connecticut, which would be near her family.

Stewart's sentencing would not come for months. Although she talked of appealing the verdict, she still had much work to complete. She started to put her business affairs in order, somehow knowing that it was important that she hand off most of her business responsibilities as she waited to see if she would go to jail. There was so much to do. Stewart's 550 employees worried that their jobs would soon be gone, as their boss pleaded with the judge that their employment was a reason that she should be kept out of jail. Stewart began to contact dozens of friends, asking them to write to the judge to ask that she remain free.[27]

Indeed, there was so much work to do to protect the company that she had built. But, if anyone could accomplish the colossal tasks at hand, it would be the super-successful businesswoman who never seemed to fail.

No one, whether they were a Martha Stewart fan or not, seemed able to imagine that the brilliant woman who had built an empire out of food and cookbooks was now going to prison. At 62 years old, though, Stewart told friends and family that she was not afraid. "She's surrounded by friends," said one longtime friend who met Stewart for dinner in the weeks after her conviction. "No one is leaving her alone."[28]

Stewart's fans across the country started to show their support in an unusual way. Martha Stewart products began to fly off the shelves. Kmart linens were selling very well, and the new Martha Stewart furniture being marketed by Bernhardt Furniture had a definite spike in sales.[29] One New Yorker, according to *People Weekly*, went out and bought $11,000 worth of furniture the weekend after the verdict was read.[30] Stewart was humbled by all of the support she received from family, friends, and fans. Even Kmart dropped the lawsuit it had filed, and the two companies announced that they had come to a new agreement regarding payments for the Martha Stewart products.[31]

Meanwhile, some of Stewart's friends recommended that she begin to work with a man who could help her reshape her business. During a dinner one evening, she was introduced to Charles Koppelman. He had worked with other high-profile people, including singer Michael Jackson and businessman Steve Madden, to reshape their images after they had run into trouble. "He had the kind of experience I needed," Stewart said.[32]

While Stewart discussed reshaping her image with Koppelman, her legal team worked at a feverish rate to try to keep her out of prison. They asked for a new trial, saying that one of the jurors lied to get on the jury. And, they looked for other ways to keep Stewart out of prison.[33] None of them worked, though. One suggestion Stewart had was that she donate time to teaching underprivileged women how to become entrepreneurs.[34] The judge did not buy that idea, either.

SENTENCED TO PRISON

When her sentencing date finally arrived in July 2004, Stewart spoke clearly to the judge. "My hopes that my life will not be completely destroyed lie entirely in your competent and experienced and merciful hands," Stewart told Judge Miriam Cedarbaum just before she was sentenced.[35] "I believe you have suffered and will continue to suffer," the judge told her.[36]

It then became clear that Stewart was, indeed, going to prison. She was given a sentence of five months, followed by five months of confinement at her new home in Bedford—the lightest sentence possible. As she and Alexis stood outside the courthouse after the sentencing, the millionaire businesswoman spoke to the television cameras, encouraging her fans and supporters to continue buying her products and subscribing to her magazine. "I'll be back," she promised, looking directly at the cameras. "I will be back."[37]

As if predicting the future, Stewart's friend, New York writer Dominick Dunne, offered his opinion to a *Time* magazine writer following the sentence. "I think she'll make the five months in prison a major life experience," Dunne suggested. "She's not going to sit and mope for five months. I bet she leaves that prison a very popular woman."[38]

In fact, Stewart was already thinking about what she would do in prison. Among the possibilities were learning to speak Italian, reading books, and writing.[39] Stewart, it seemed, would have her prison stay planned as much as possible.

CHARLES KOPPELMAN

When Martha Stewart teamed with Donald Trump and Mark Burnett in 2005 to produce *The Apprentice: Martha Stewart*, she chose two people to be her sidekicks to keep tabs on the contestants competing for the title.

One was her daughter, Alexis Stewart. The other was Charles Koppelman, the chairman of the board of Martha Stewart Living Omnimedia. Koppelman and Stewart were casual acquaintances before Stewart was convicted. While some of her friends were abandoning her, Koppelman wanted to help her and invited her to dinner. He knew that, despite her serious troubles, many people still respected her achievements. He thought that her career and business could be saved even while she was in prison.

Koppelman, who was born in 1940 in Brooklyn, had experience working to reshape the images of famous people. In particular, he played an important role with Steve Madden's popular shoe company when Madden was in prison for 41 months for fraud.

But first, Koppelman made his name in the music world. In 1960, he and two college friends at Adelphi University on Long Island, New York, started a group called The Ivy Three. They had a hit called "Yogi," about the cartoon bear, which peaked in the Top Ten on the *Billboard* charts. He soon got into the business side of the music industry and eventually formed S.B.K. Entertainment World, which became the world's largest independent music publisher. In 1989, it merged with EMI Music, making

The evening after her sentencing, she dined with Alexis and a friend at a Manhattan restaurant. Again, family and friends helped to comfort her in this very difficult time.

it the biggest music publishing sale at the time. Along the way, he worked with such greats as Billy Joel, Barbra Streisand, Dolly Parton, Lionel Richie, the Four Tops, Cher, and Diana Ross.

Koppelman helped launch and re-image many careers. In 1990, he persuaded Robert Van Winkle to wear an odd hair-cut and baggy pants—and change his name to Vanilla Ice. His debut single, "Ice Ice Baby," sold 17 million copies, and Vanilla Ice became famous as the first white rap star. Three years later, Koppelman gave the legendary Frank Sinatra one final smash album by pairing him with younger singers. The album, *Duets*, was one of Sinatra's best-selling recordings. Koppelman also worked with Michael Jackson when the superstar was having financial troubles.

In a story in the *Los Angeles Times*, Koppelman said, "No matter what anybody says, all that matters to me is the music. What people forget is our business starts with the music. If you have the belief in your gut about a song and artist, you have to have the nerve to stand behind the thing, to stay the course."*

After that dinner with Martha Stewart, Koppelman oversaw her company, becoming chairman of the board in June 2005. Some of his ideas included publishing a book about Stewart's business tips and getting Stewart her own channel on Sirius, the satellite radio company.

---

*Chuck Philips, "How Things Really Stack Up at the Capitol Records Tower," *Los Angeles Times*, June 13, 1993.

A throng of reporters and cameramen surrounded Martha Stewart on July 16, 2004, outside federal court in Manhattan after she was sentenced to five months in prison. "I'll be back," a determined Martha Stewart promised.

The following night she cooked bluestone crabs with her mother, and they were joined for dinner by one of her brothers.[40]

As the most unusual summer in Stewart's life drew to a close, she was having second thoughts about dragging out the process. Stewart began to contemplate serving her prison term even as her appeal moved forward. "She's giving very serious consideration to going ahead and serving her incarceration sentence for the good of the company, so she can put the issue behind her," one of her attorneys said.[41]

With the stress of the trial and her sentencing over, Stewart tried to get back into a routine. She started to exercise more and put herself on a diet. She was spotted at a few parties around the Hamptons, including one at the estate of successful businessman Calvin Klein.

Indeed, just a few weeks later, Stewart announced an important decision. From a stage in her New York City design center and test kitchen, she announced that she would begin her prison sentence as soon as possible. Dressed in a beige outfit and surrounded by the top people in her company, Stewart was matter of fact. "I have decided to serve my sentence now, to put this behind me and get on with my life and living as soon as possible," she said. "I know that I have a very tough five months ahead of me, but I understand, too, that I will get through those months knowing that I have the ability to return to my productive and normal life."[42]

With that and a bit of light discussion that followed, Stewart walked off the stage. By now, the ordeal had spanned more than two-and-a-half years. A new stage in Martha Stewart's life was about to begin.

A WEST VIRGINIA PRISON

It was a crisp fall day when Stewart arrived at the prison to which she was finally assigned. The Alderson Federal Prison Camp is a minimum-security facility in an isolated valley in the southern West Virginia mountains. It wasn't the penitentiary in Danville, Connecticut, where everyone assumed Stewart would be. Although it was several hours outside New York City, the prison was at least near the East Coast.

Treated no differently from other incoming inmates, Stewart underwent a mandatory strip search and was issued khaki slacks and T-shirts. She was assigned the bottom bunk in a cubicle. The cottage in which she was housed held 59 other inmates. Alexis and one of the top editors from *Martha Stewart Living* spent much of that first weekend with her, playing games like Scrabble in a visitors' area that was packed with other inmates, their families, and friends. It was that weekend, when Alexis ran out of coins to buy food in the visitors' lounge, that probably stuck in Stewart's mind as she advised other visitors over the next several months to be sure to bring plenty of quarters with them.[43]

"She smiles at everyone," one man reported to *People Weekly*, after seeing Stewart at Alderson that weekend while he was visiting his girlfriend there.[44]

Despite having millions of dollars and being much more well off than most of the other inmates, Stewart was only permitted to spend $290 a month in the prison commissary, where she could buy snacks and other necessities like toothpaste and deodorant. Once, when she tried to get additional money during a telephone call with her assistant so that she could help some of the poorest inmates, a third voice immediately told her to hang up the phone. A prison official, whose job it was to listen in on inmates' phone calls, knew Stewart was asking for something that was against the rules. Despite her wealth, she was not allowed to give money to any of the inmates.[45]

Like other inmates, though, Stewart was expected to hold a prison job. She earned a little bit of money each week by cleaning the warden's offices. Every day, she dusted and scrubbed from 7:30 A.M. to 3:30 P.M.[46]

Although she was apparently very frustrated with the situation, Stewart had prepared herself as much as possible for the months of prison that she would endure. As always, she believed that having the right mind-set could help a person in the most challenging of situations. "I can almost bend steel with my mind," she had told talk-show host Oprah Winfrey during an interview years earlier. "I can bend anything if I try hard enough. I can make myself do almost anything."[47] At the time, who would ever have

Representatives of the media staked out the entrance to the Alderson Federal Prison Camp in West Virginia on October 6, 2004—two days before Martha Stewart would report there to start her jail term.

thought that Martha Stewart would need to figure out how to live in prison?

Weeks after she went into prison, Stewart's 90-year-old mother arrived for a visit on Thanksgiving Day with Stewart's youngest sister and her family. "It was a big relief for all of us to see Martha so healthy, well-adjusted, and well-liked," Stewart's sister told a reporter after the visit.[48]

While in prison, Stewart exercised regularly and meditated. She made friends with other inmates, including drug dealers, a peace activist who was convicted after protesting at a missile silo, and others. She was touched to discover how little support some inmates had from either family or friends. And, in some cases, she set out to befriend women whom she thought she could help.

During the Christmas holidays, Stewart and the inmates made decorations for their cottage and for some of the prison staff. Her cottage competed for an annual decoration award, but she was probably disappointed that her group did not win. Still, she found other projects to engage her busy mind. She crocheted small animals that she planned to give to her pets when she returned home.[49] On New Year's Eve, she asked inmates to her room for a small party.[50]

Despite its founder's incarceration, Martha Stewart Living Omnimedia seemed to be surviving quite well. Kmart announced that it would be taking over Sears, Roebuck & Co., with the buyout immediately creating more wealth for Stewart. The staff in New York stayed busy without the company's founder in town, even beginning negotiations with NBC for a new syndicated series in which Stewart would be featured.[51]

Before entering prison, Stewart had discussions with producer Mark Burnett, who had created the television programs *Survivor* and *The Apprentice*. He suggested producing programs together, and Stewart had listened, looking forward to the day when she could start a new television program. Even though Stewart was not allowed to work while in prison, Burnett still visited just to check in.[52]

When the chimes struck the new year, Martha Stewart knew that, unlike many of the other women at the Alderson penitentiary, she would be returning home soon. In the next few months, before her release, she tackled the task of planning the spring garden she would plant at her Bedford estate. Stewart had earned respect from many as she showed true grace, by taking her punishment, going to jail sooner than she needed to, and then emerging months later in time to plant her spring garden. Just before she was released, Stewart and about 25 other prisoners held a pot-luck dinner. Martha Stewart, the creator of dozens of cookbooks, prepared nachos for the event.[53]

Martha Stewart's Rebirth

Martha Stewart left Alderson in the dead of night during the early morning hours of March 4, 2005. As a few well-wishers waved signs saying goodbye, Stewart was accompanied by Alexis as they boarded a private 10-seat plane and flew out of the tiny airport that was several miles from the prison gate. Stewart wore a gray poncho that had been knitted by a fellow inmate and given to her as a gift.

It had been a long, reflective winter at Alderson. Stewart had learned about local culture, even gathering dandelion greens and crab apples from the prison grounds to make salads and other dishes. It was a stunning reality, most likely, for Stewart to spend five nearly idle months with a group of women with whom she had little in common. Still, Stewart created friendships and bonds that she said would affect her for many years to come.

Stewart flew to her home in Bedford, New York, where she would continue to serve her sentence. By now the value of the refurbished estate was estimated at $40 million[1]—it was a drastic change from the barren walls of a federal penitentiary. Wearing an ankle bracelet, Stewart was permitted to leave Bedford's premises for only 48 hours a week for work-related activities. But, certainly, there was work to be done on the house and gardens during the hours she would spend at home.

The first morning after arriving at home, Stewart went outdoors to feed her horses and visit the pets she had missed so much while being away. In a quilted jacket and matching scarf, she wandered the grounds and even took compassion that chilly morning on the media representatives who had staked out her house—serving hot chocolate to the reporters and photographers who were trying to cover this ongoing drama. "I'm dreaming of cappuccino," she confided in them.[2]

BACK TO THE OFFICE

That weekend, family and friends came and went. Martha served dinner a few times and her longtime hairstylist showed up to give her a new look. The following Monday, just before getting her ankle bracelet fitted, she was accompanied by Alexis as she met with nearly 500 employees of Martha Stewart Living Omnimedia at their Manhattan office. Stewart also wrote a note on her company Web site, speaking to her fans. "The experience of the last five months … has been life-altering and life-affirming," she said. "My heart is filled with joy at the prospect of the warm embraces of my family, friends, and colleagues."[3]

On her first day home after her release from prison, Martha Stewart spent a little time with her horses. A few days later, she traveled to Manhattan to meet with the nearly 500 employees of Martha Stewart Living Omnimedia. Under her sentence, Stewart could only leave her home for 48 hours each week for the next five months.

Stewart very quickly integrated herself back in the mainstream of her busy life. Despite being able to leave Bedford for only two days a week, there seemed to be no stopping the woman who had built a business kingdom. Just a few months after her release, Stewart attended the pre-Emmy Awards ceremony where her defunct program, *Martha Stewart Living*, won in a category called "outstanding service show." Thus, Stewart obviously enjoyed the irony of the event.[4]

"These five months have really brought a new dimension to her life," producer Mark Burnett told a reporter from *People Weekly*. "Here is a 63-year-old woman who did her time with a really positive outlook. She'd be great on *Survivor*."[5]

Even before Stewart was released, Burnett had started to schedule auditions for those who would seek the position of being Stewart's apprentice on a new program called *The Apprentice: Martha Stewart*.[6] The program was scheduled to be shown, with Stewart in the starring role, later in the fall. Certainly, this busy woman was only about to get busier.

Meanwhile, Martha Stewart Living Omnimedia had done well. For the second time in her life, the company stock value had increased enough to make Stewart a billionaire. Besides planning *The Apprentice* with Burnett, she was developing a new daily program, called *The Martha Stewart Show*. And, she continued to launch new products for Kmart and Bernhardt furniture.[7] Stewart also prepared to launch her own *Martha Stewart Living* radio channel on Sirius Satellite Radio and planned to publish a business book called *The Martha Rules*, a guide for entrepreneurs.[8]

"My goal with this book is to help people turn their passions into successful businesses, as I did myself through many of the things I learned over the years," Stewart said. "While the advice I impart in the book was developed through my own experiences as an entrepreneur, many of the examples I provide can apply to anyone about how to start or build or expand a venture, whether it is a business, a philanthropic endeavor, or a personal improvement program."[9]

Everyone seemed interested—and even in awe of—Stewart's re-entry into life. "The fact is, the American public loves a great comeback," said Jeff Zucker, president of NBC. "And her story is even more compelling now."[10]

Certainly, at this point in her life, Stewart needed the support of many other people. Eventually, a woman named Susan Lyne, who was a former ABC television executive, replaced Sharon Patrick, the woman Stewart had deemed her successor at Martha Stewart Living Omnimedia. Lyne would be among Stewart's best allies as she re-entered public life.

Donald Trump, who created *The Apprentice* with Burnett, also became a huge supporter. "Thanks to the enduring appeal of her magazine and earlier TV programs, Martha is still the standard for gracious living," Trump wrote in *Time* magazine. "She gave value and definition to a niche that had been underappreciated. Her influence on American culture is enormous."[11]

Soon after getting out of prison, Stewart was named one of "The 50 Most Beautiful People" by *People Weekly*. She had an extensive interview with a reporter regarding her health regimen while she was in prison and after she got out. Among her top tips were exercising, eating healthy foods, not indulging in alcohol or much caffeine, and staying active. Stewart reported that she had spent much time walking Alderson's 100 acres, exercising in its fitness room, and teaching yoga classes. Years earlier, Alexis had introduced her to yoga, and Stewart found it helpful in maintaining flexibility and relaxation. By the time she was released from prison, after following a simple health regime, Stewart had dropped 20 pounds (9 kilograms).[12] Perhaps some of that had to do with the fact that she was not very fond of the prison food.

Support for Stewart, the former inmate, came from other interesting places, too. Even though *Martha Stewart Living* struggled to regain advertisers that it had lost during Stewart's prison ordeal, some major companies still offered their endorsement. "The women who read Martha Stewart are not concerned about the controversy," said a spokeswoman for the Estée Lauder cosmetics company. "They believe in her, and they believe in her products."[13]

Not everyone loved Martha Stewart, though. Some people still complained that, despite going to prison, Stewart never admitted that she was guilty of the charges brought against her. But, there was a reason why Stewart did not admit guilt. Just because she was out of prison did not mean that she was trouble-free. There was still a complaint filed against her by the U.S. Securities and Exchange Commission, which was trying to ban Stewart from ever being a director or an officer in a public company, including the one that bears her name. Stewart had decided that she would fight this charge.[14] By late 2006, Stewart had made a deal with the Securities and Exchange Commission to pay $195,000 if her ban from serving as an officer in a public company was limited to only five years.[15] That means that in 2011 Stewart would be able to hold an important title with her own company again.

Stewart was more than ready to move beyond those cold winter months spent in southern West Virginia and all of the court battles she had experienced in the previous few years. "I've survived a very, very difficult challenge," she said. "Fair or not, it's over—almost—and we're just going to try to proceed on our merry way."[16]

As Stewart's first summer outside of prison wore on, she looked forward to getting her ankle bracelet removed and to getting on with her life. Weeks later, she would say that being on home confinement was more difficult than being in prison. "You have to watch the clock constantly because you're only allowed out of your home for a limited period, and for a busy person, watching the clock, and knowing other people are watching the clock, is extremely difficult,"[17] she said.

Stewart looked forward to the beginning of her new daily television program *The Martha Stewart Show*—which was touted as a chance to show off her rarely seen sense of humor. In the meantime, the U.S. Probation Office in New York City questioned some of Stewart's activities—such as attending a yoga class. "She is always claiming to be working," the chief probation officer said.[18]

Who says that Martha Stewart has no sense of humor? During a news conference to promote her two new TV shows, Stewart revealed her ankle bracelet to those in attendance. With her was television producer Mark Burnett. Stewart said that, in some ways, home confinement and the ankle bracelet were harder to deal with than her time in prison.

In fact, despite the limitations she endured, Stewart *was* always working. Besides her new daily television program, she was getting ready to launch her 24-hour lifestyle channel with Sirius, she was overseeing a new home improvement show for the Discovery Channel, and she was working on *The Apprentice*. In addition, her new business advice book would soon be released, and she was working on a holiday music CD set that would also contain some of her special recipes.[19]

Even with her busy schedule, when August 3 rolled around, she celebrated her sixty-fourth birthday with a small party. The kitchen in Stewart's Bedford home was very large and shiny with its marble countertops and stainless steel cabinets. The renovation had been big, with the kitchen replacing six original smaller rooms and hallways. "I really wanted an airy and open kitchen, with professional cooking equipment, seating, a built-in home office and media center, and a spot for each of the luxuries I coveted, such as a large espresso machine and a panini iron for making pressed Italian sandwiches, plus a spacious glass-doored refrigerator and a stainless-steel-doored freezer," Stewart wrote in a posting on her Web site.[20] The evening of her birthday, Stewart's new personal chef prepared a Spanish menu, featuring tapas, gazpacho, and paella, a rice dish that often features seafood.[21]

PROMOTING HER SHOWS

Back on the media circuit, Stewart made several guest appearances to promote her new shows and to talk about her plans for the future. Certainly, this was challenging after the public humiliation of being sent to prison. "Somehow I have managed to build a very fine company with a very fine work force filled with people who are still there from the earliest days," she told a reporter for *Time* as she was promoting *The Apprentice: Martha Stewart*. "I can be fair and decisive and encouraging as well as demanding, and those are the characteristics you'll see on *The Apprentice*."[22]

In the meantime, Stewart's ankle bracelet was removed, and she began 18 months of probation, which meant she had to meet regularly with her probation officer. Even though Stewart was already wealthy enough and successful enough to retire and never appear on television or in her magazine again, she would not quit. She was out to prove that she could still gain respect for her wisdom, not only regarding domestic issues but also regarding her business. Perhaps she was out to prove to those people who still did not believe that Martha Stewart was capable of being successful despite the obstacles she had had to overcome in her life.

Through the fall, the reviews of *The Apprentice: Martha Stewart* were less than flattering, but weeks later Stewart was listed as No. 21 on *Fortune* magazine's 2005 Most Powerful Women list. Ad sales for *Martha Stewart Living* were vastly improving, and her book, *The Martha Rules*, made it onto the *New York Times* bestseller list. [23]

Even though stock prices for Martha Stewart Living Omnimedia had fallen again, she still had stock valued at $500 million. Later that year when NBC refused to pick up *The Apprentice: Martha Stewart* for a second season, there was a heated, public debate between Stewart and Trump about who was responsible for the show's failure. In the end, Stewart moved on and left Trump and Burnett with their show.

Despite Trump's taunts that her new daily program would also struggle, *The Martha Stewart Show* was nominated for five Daytime Emmy awards in 2006 and four in 2007, including outstanding show and outstanding host. But mainly because of the falling stock price of Martha Stewart Living Omnimedia, Stewart was taken off the *Forbes* list of the 400 wealthiest businesspeople.[24]

Some people were now saying that Stewart was overexposed because she had re-entered public life in a very prominent way. Stewart quietly worked to build better bonds with potential advertisers, entertaining a stream of supporters with intimate dinners at her Bedford home. Fortunately, her chef was there to do most of the cooking.[25]

NEW DEALS

Stewart did not stop thinking about new partnerships, either. On one short business trip, she visited the headquarters of KB Home in North Carolina[26] and eventually decided to partner with the company to produce a line of Martha Stewart homes. Within several months, more than 3,800 homes had been sold, perhaps proving that the Martha Stewart brand was, in fact, untarnished.

Instead of running out of ideas, Stewart seemed to have more. For a short time, she started another magazine called *Blueprint*, which was aimed at women 25 to 45 years old, but it was taken off the market after only a few issues. She talked with a winemaker in California and started to produce a wine called Martha Stewart Vintage.[27] On the twenty-fifth anniversary of the publication of her first book, *Entertaining*, she planned a special program on her television show, featuring some of Stewart's friends from her catering days. Stewart shared desserts that were featured in the book, including the Clementine Tart, Pear Frangipane Tart, and Lemon Curd Tartlets.

She partnered with Macy's department store on a new line of home products in 2007, in addition to creating new products for other stores that included paints, rugs, food, carpet tiles, and craft materials.[28] Martha Stewart Living Omnimedia also announced that it would purchase the company owned by renowned New Orleans chef Emeril Lagasse for more than $45 million.[29] And Stewart had also put her name on a line of sewing machines produced by another company. "I think sewing is such an important thing to know and especially to teach kids," Stewart said. "It's important to be thrifty."[30]

EMERIL LAGASSE

The kid who grew up in the small town of Fall River, Massachusetts, is now a first-name-only celebrity chef on the Food Network known for his signature exclamation: "Bam!"

The culinary career of Emeril Lagasse began when he was a teenager working at a Portuguese bakery, learning about breads and pastries. After graduating from high school, he turned down a full scholarship to the New England Conservatory of Music so he could try to become a professional chef. He spent years studying and working in Europe and the United States before landing in New Orleans as executive chef at the famous Commander's Palace.

After more than seven years building a reputation, Lagasse opened his own establishment, which he called Emeril's, in 1990. It was a quick success. In fact, that same year, the New Orleans establishment was named Best Restaurant of the Year by *Esquire* magazine.

From there, Lagasse's star only got brighter. He won the prestigious James Beard Award as Best Southeast Chef in 1991, opened a second New Orleans restaurant the following year, and published his first cookbook, *"New" New Orleans Cooking*, in 1993.

By 1995, Emeril had opened a third restaurant—a fish house in the MGM Grand Casino in Las Vegas—and he started *Essence of Emeril*, a cooking show on the Food Network. He became a superstar and a household name with his imaginative dishes and exuberant personality. (He would yell "Bam!" to make a point

In the fall of 2007, hundreds of fans awaited Stewart and her mother as they arrived at the Macy's flagship store at Herald Square in Manhattan to launch the new Martha

about one of his recipes). *Time* magazine voted *Essence of Emeril* one of the top 10 shows of the year in 1996. By 2008, he had hosted more than 1,600 shows, reaching more than 85 million homes daily.

Through the years he has opened more restaurants and published more books. Besides Las Vegas and New Orleans, his restaurants are now in Orlando; Atlanta; Gulfport, Mississippi; and Miami Beach. Among his 12 books—which have sold more than 2.5 million copies—is a children's cookbook called *There's a Chef in My Soup*. He has also started various cooking lines: cutlery, California wines, seasonings, salad dressings, and pasta sauces. In 2006, Lagasse developed meals for NASA astronauts that were served in space. He even starred in his own NBC comedy called *Emeril*, which debuted in 2001 but did not last very long.

His empire continued to grow. By early 2008, he was opening more restaurants and working on a new TV program called *Emeril Green* on the Planet Green channel. But he also sold much of his culinary business to Martha Stewart Living Omnimedia.

Lagasse has established the Emeril Lagasse Foundation, which helps expose children, particularly those struggling with poverty or other disadvantages, to various opportunities, especially involving cooking or the hospitality business. Each fall, he holds a fundraiser in New Orleans to raise money for children. In 2007, the event raised more than $2 million.

Stewart line of dishes, linens, and more. "I just had a dinner party for 32 with my own creamware (dishes)," Stewart told a writer for *The Washington Post*. "I bought 36 of everything in that line."[31]

As a surprise, dozens of audience members at *The Martha Stewart Show* were put on a bus and given $250 gift cards to use at Macy's that day. It was the opening day for the third season of Stewart's new show, and she was certainly ready to celebrate.

PERSONAL LOSS

Her excitement during the next few months was outweighed, though, by the death of one of the most important people in her life. Stewart's mother, Martha Kostyra, died at the age of 93. The small woman had been called Big Martha by family members for many years, even though her famous daughter towered over her when she made regular appearances on Martha's television show to teach viewers to make traditional Polish recipes and other family favorites. While Stewart was in prison, Big Martha was a devoted mother, spending time with the pets at Stewart's home and traveling hundreds of miles to visit her incarcerated daughter. But in early November 2007, Kostyra suffered a stroke that made it hard to move the left side of her body. When she died on November 16, the entire family was very sad.

"A loss like this is always hard to assimilate into daily life, and each of Mother's six children will learn to cope with her dying in a different way," Stewart wrote on her Web site and in a column that was published in her magazine. "Personally, I will miss our weekly visits and our several-times-a-week phone calls—and I will miss the thoughtful cards mother sent every holiday and birthday, without fail."[32]

Even though she had lost one of her most important influences, Stewart's life continued to blossom. By mid-March in

2008, Stewart was joined by a crowd of followers when she cut the ribbon to Macy's 34th Annual Flower Show in New York City. That same week, Stewart and comedian Conan O'Brien met a few times—first on his late-night comedy show and then on her daytime show. In the meantime, after cutting the ribbon, Stewart smiled and greeted fans who stopped by to have her sign copies of her new books, *Martha Stewart's Cookies* and *Martha Stewart's Wedding Cakes*.[33]

On her Web site that week, Stewart posted pictures of her three dogs—Francesca, Paw Paw, and Sharkey—as they played in the yard. The younger two dogs frolicked about while the older Paw Paw ambled around watching them. Inside the house, Stewart posed Francesca and Sharkey on her marble kitchen countertops and took more pictures.[34]

It wasn't long after that day that Stewart was saddened again, though. Paw Paw, the 60-pound (27-kilogram) chow that had been her faithful companion for many years, died. Stewart's chows had recently been the stars of her television show, during an episode in which all the audience members also brought their dogs. At the time of his death, Paw Paw was quite old—13. "Paw Paw was a spectacular chow and

IN HER OWN WORDS

After her mother's death in November 2007, Martha Stewart wrote about one of the comforts her mother had provided:

> I will miss the cotton-flannel nightgowns she sewed for me almost every year—nightgowns that were long enough to wrap my feet in while I slept, with sleeves long enough for my long arms.

Martha Stewart appeared at Macy's flagship department store in Manhattan in March 2008 for the ribbon cutting for the store's 34th Annual Flower Show. She was also promoting two of her new books, *Martha Stewart's Wedding Cakes* and *Martha Stewart's Cookies*.

an even more spectacular dog," a sad Stewart wrote on her blog. "He was always my loyal companion displaying the most agreeable temperament."[35]

RISING TO THE CHALLENGE

Martha Stewart's tenacious ability to bounce back from the most unsettling of circumstances served her well during such trying days. Despite the most difficult challenges, this tough-minded woman is never seen crying in public. And, even though she has been accused of losing patience at times, Stewart always stays focused on her core mission—providing homemakers with fresh, creative ideas that enhance the lives of their families and friends.

With a large staff that offers much support, she continues to devote her life to her television show, radio programming, magazines, books, and other products. On her Web site in the spring, she posted new pictures of the guesthouse at her Maine property, freshly decorated all in pale pinks. Even though many years have passed since her first domestic endeavors, Stewart still takes great pleasure in the simple process of choosing fresh colors for rooms in her homes.

A few months later, she entertained new cookbook author Virginia Willis—a former employee—as Willis whipped up an angel food cake on Stewart's TV show in honor of Mother's Day. With a delectable crème anglaise sauce on the cake and the audience thrilled with copies of the new cookbook, Stewart moved on to talk about fresh floral arrangements and the creation of a community garden in New York, designed and funded by the Martha Stewart Living Omnimedia Foundation. The foundation was established to enhance the lives of women and children. During this segment on her television show, she shared her love of gardening and urged her viewers to create community projects of their own to beautify areas that may be downtrodden.

Stewart's celebration of mothers wasn't over yet, though, as a few days later she offered more ideas to honor mom, including the recipe for creating a chocolate clutch purse. Stewart's enthusiasm for sharing new and creative ideas never seemed to diminish.

Certainly, her creativity has served her well. Once a Westport housewife who catered affairs out of her home, she has become a domestic brand builder and a proven national phenomenon. If Martha Stewart were to retire today, she would live a very well-off lifestyle. Still, she forges onward, planning more television shows, creating more partnerships, and enjoying the rich and fulfilling life to which she has become accustomed.

CHRONOLOGY

1941   Martha Kostyra is born on August 3 in Jersey City, New Jersey.

1961   Marries Andy Stewart during her sophomore year at Barnard College.

1965   Daughter Alexis Stewart is born.

1967   Begins career as a stockbroker; she is one of the few women at the time working on Wall Street.

1971   The Stewarts purchase a home in Westport, Connecticut.

1973   Quits her job as a stockbroker; she and her family move to Westport; soon she begins a catering business.

1982   Publishes her first book, *Entertaining*.

1987   Signs contract with Kmart to act as a consultant and to design products for the retailer.

1990   *Martha Stewart Living* magazine is launched; she and Andy Stewart divorce.

1993   The TV show *Martha Stewart Living* debuts.

1995   Persuades Time Inc. to create a subsidiary, Martha Stewart Living Enterprises; is named CEO of the subsidiary.

1996   Is named one of *Time* magazine's 25 Most Influential Americans.

1997   Purchases Martha Stewart Living Enterprises from Time Inc., renaming the company Martha Stewart Living Omnimedia.

1998   *Martha Stewart Living* is the top-ranked daily syndicated TV series; Stewart is named among *Forbes* magazine's 50 Most Powerful Women.

1999   Martha Stewart Living Omnimedia goes public; Stewart purchases a 152-acre estate in Bedford, New York.

2002   Becomes the target of an investigation into the sale of stock she owned in a biotechnology company called ImClone.

2003   Stewart is indicted in federal court on charges of securities fraud, obstruction of justice, and conspiracy.

2004   Stewart is convicted of the charges against her; begins to serve her five-month sentence in October at the Alderson Federal Prison Camp in West Virginia.

2005   Upon her release from prison, she serves five months of home confinement in Bedford, New York; launches her second daily television series, *The Martha Stewart Show*; stars in *The Apprentice: Martha Stewart*.

2007   Partners with Macy's department store; her mother, Martha Kostyra, dies in November at age 93.

2008   Celebrates the 500th episode of *The Martha Stewart Show*.

NOTES

CHAPTER 1: THE DOMESTIC DIVA

1. "Martha Stewart," Portfolio.com. Available online at http://www.portfolio.com/resources/executive-profiles/Martha-Stewart-25369.
2. "Martha Stewart Biography," FoxNews.com. Available online at http://www.foxnews.com/story/0,2933,193645,00.html?sPage=fnc/entertainment/celebrity/stewart.
3. Adam Lashinsky, "Managing Martha," *Fortune*, June 10, 2002.
4. "Martha Stewart Biography," FoxNews.com.
5. Jill Gerston, "Life Is Just a Bowl of Rhubarb Crisp (And So Easy!)," *New York Times*, October 9, 1994.
6. *The Martha Stewart Show*, December 31, 2007.
7. Gerston, "Life Is Just a Bowl of Rhubarb Crisp (And So Easy!)."
8. June Weir, "Taking Her Show on the Road: 'Queen of Home' Martha Stewart Looks to Interactive Media," *Advertising Age*, August 22, 1994.
9. Lisa LaMotta, "Martha and Emeril: Cozy in the Kitchen," *Forbes*, February 19, 2008.
10. "Biography: Martha Stewart—Multimedia Lifestyle Entrepreneur," Academy of Achievement Web site. Available online at http://www.achievement.org/autodoc/page/ste0bio-1.
11. Gerston, "Life Is Just a Bowl of Rhubarb Crisp (And So Easy!)."
12. Ibid.
13. Virginia Heffernan, "Martha Makes Merry," *Slate*, December 5, 2002.

CHAPTER 2: A BIG FAMILY

1. "Biography: Martha Stewart—Multimedia Lifestyle Entrepreneur," Academy of Achievement Web site.
2. Martha Stewart, "Remembering: At Home with Big Martha," *Martha Stewart Living*, February 2004, p. 164.
3. Martha Stewart, "Remembering," *Martha Stewart Living*, October 2002, p. 316.
4. Martha Stewart, "From My Home to Yours—Summer's Best Flavor: Tomatoes," *Martha Stewart Living*, July 2005, p. 21.
5. Martha Stewart, *Martha Stewart's Quick Cook Menus*. New York: Clarkson Potter, 1988, p. 31.
6. Stewart, "Remembering: At Home with Big Martha."
7. Stewart, "Remembering," October 2002.
8. Margaret Roach, "Mother Knows Best," *Martha Stewart Living*, February 2004, p. 92.
9. Martha Stewart, "Remembering: Cozy Comfort," *Martha Stewart Living*, January 2004, p. 160.
10. Martha Stewart, "Remembering," *Martha Stewart Living*, August 2002, p. 224.

11. Jerry Oppenheimer, "The Imperfect Life of Miss Perfect," *Toronto Sun*, July 20, 1997.
12. Martha Stewart, "Remembering," *Martha Stewart Living*, August 2003, p. 184.
13. Heffernan, "Martha Makes Merry."
14. Roach, "Mother Knows Best."
15. "Interview: Martha Stewart—Multimedia Lifestyle Entrepreneur," Academy of Achievement Web site, June 2, 1995. Available online at http://www.achievement.org/autodoc/page/ste0int-1.
16. Ibid.
17. Ibid.
18. Martha Stewart, *Entertaining*. New York: Clarkson Potter, 1982, p. 1.
19. Mary Elizabeth Williams, "Salon Brilliant Careers: She's Martha and You're Not," *Salon*, February 1999.
20. Oprah Winfrey, "Oprah's Cut with Martha Stewart." *O, the Oprah Magazine*, September 2000.
21. Michelle Green, "The Best Revenge—for Martha Stewart, Living Well May Be Much, Much More Than a Vast Cottage Industry," *People Weekly*, October 2, 1995.
22. "Interview: Martha Stewart—Multimedia Lifestyle Entrepreneur," Academy of Achievement Web site.
23. Stewart, *Martha Stewart's Quick Cook Menus*, p. 95.
24. Stewart, *Entertaining*, p. 10.
25. Joan Didion, "Everywoman.com," *New Yorker*, February 21, 2000.
26. "Biography: Martha Stewart—Multimedia Lifestyle Entrepreneur," Academy of Achievement Web site.

CHAPTER 3: A MODEL WOMAN

1. Adam Lashinsky, "Managing Martha." *Fortune*, June 10, 2002, p. 46.
2. Ibid.
3. Charlotte Beers, Martha Stewart, and Darla Moore, "Cocktails at Charlotte's with Martha and Darla," *Fortune*, August 5, 1996.
4. "Interview: Martha Stewart—Multimedia Lifestyle Entrepreneur," Academy of Achievement Web site.
5. Stewart, *Martha Stewart's Quick Cook Menus*, p. 159.
6. Martha Stewart, "Remembering Turkey Hill," *Martha Stewart Living*, October 2007, p. 191.
7. Ibid.
8. Ibid.
9. Donald Trump, "The Domestic Diva Is Back," *Time*, April 18, 2005.
10. Cynthia Tucker, "Why They're Picking on Martha," *Time*, June 16, 2003.

11. Patricia Leigh Brown, "The Perfect Wedding: Only Tears of Joy," *New York Times*, April 4, 1987.
12. Ibid.
13. Ibid.
14. Stewart, *Martha Stewart's Quick Cook Menus*, inside front flap.
15 Ibid., p. 46.
16. Deirdre Donahue, "Stewart's Gold Touch," *USA Today*, December 18, 1989.

CHAPTER 4: PERFECTLY ENTERTAINING

1. Ibid.
2. Ibid.
3. Ibid.
4. Ibid.
5. Ibid.
6. Martha Stewart, "From My Home to Yours: The First Fifteen Years," *Martha Stewart Living*, January 2006.
7. Ibid.
8. Green, "The Best Revenge."
9. Deirdre Carmody, "The Media Business: Martha Stewart Gains a Fan: Time Warner," *New York Times*, May 27, 1991.
10. "Martha Stewart Gets TV Show," *Advertising Age*, January 25, 1993.
11. Robin DeRosa, "For Martha Stewart, Life Is for Nothing but 'Living'," *USA Today*, December 15, 1993.
12. Ibid.
13. Green, "The Best Revenge."
14. Ibid.
15. Gerston, "Life Is Just a Bowl of Rhubarb Crisp (And So Easy!)."
16. Brendan Gill, "The Weekend House," *New Yorker*, October 16, 1995.
17. Green, "The Best Revenge."
18. Richard Z. Chesnoff, "The Real Joy of Cooking," *U.S. News & World Report*, September 25, 1995.
19. Renee Graham, "Martha Stewart Shows Up (and on) 'Ellen'," *The Boston Globe*, November 15, 1995.
20. "Time 25: Time's 25 Most Influential Americans," *Time*, June 17, 1996.
21. Rick Marin, "Be-Marthas, Do-Marthas, and Beyond Martha: Add a Christmas Special to Her Omnimedia Empire," *Newsweek*, December 11, 1995.
22. Diana Aitchison, "A Few Minutes with Martha," *St. Petersburg Times*, January 13, 1991.
23. Marin, "Be-Marthas, Do-Marthas, and Beyond Martha."
24. Green, "The Best Revenge."

CHAPTER 5: BUILDING AN OMNI-BUSINESS

1. "Martha Stewart," *People Weekly*, May 6, 1996.
2. Beers, Stewart, and Moore, "Cocktails at Charlotte's with Martha and Darla."
3. Naomi Tajitsu, "Martha Stewart Pinpoints Japanese Market," *Daily Yomiuri* (Tokyo, Japan), November 18, 2000.
4. Angela K. King, "Right Time for Martha to Control Her Empire," *Daily News* (New York), February 5, 1997.
5. Miriam Horn, "Martha Stewart Living Large—Retailing," *U.S. News & World Report*, March 3, 1997.
6. Martha Stewart, *Good Things*. New York: Martha Stewart Living Omnimedia, 1997, p. 20.
7. Robin Pogrebin, "Master of Her Own Destiny," *New York Times*, February 8, 1998.
8. "Ford, Mercury Sign Martha Stewart Deal," *Automotive Age*, September 7, 1998.
9. Keith J. Kelly, "More Martha Stewart on TV is OK'd," *Advertising Age*, August 26, 1996.
10. Pogrebin, "Master of Her Own Destiny."
11. Martha Stewart, *Decorating for the Holidays*. New York: Martha Stewart Living Omnimedia, 1998, p. 14.
12. Pogrebin, "Master of Her Own Destiny."
13. Ibid.

CHAPTER 6: A POWERFUL FORCE

1. Martha Stewart, *Christmas with Martha Stewart Living*. New York: Martha Stewart Living Omnimedia, 1997, p. 9.
2. "A Dress Code Drama," *People Weekly*, June 28, 1999.
3. Ibid.
4. Martha Stewart, "A Letter from Martha," *Martha Stewart Living*, December 1999, p. 20.
5. Anne-Marie O'Neill and Sue Miller, "Martha's Midas Touch," *People Weekly*, December 13, 1999.
6. Ibid.
7. Ibid.
8. Peg Tyre, "Will Martha Make a Move?" *Newsweek*, January 28, 2002.
9. O'Neill and Miller, "Martha's Midas Touch."
10. Merri Rosenberg, "For Martha Stewart, a 152-Acre Estate in Katonah," *New York Times*, November 12, 2000.
11. Elizabeth Maker, "Martha Stewart Tip: Feng Shui with Fur," *New York Times*, February 24, 2002.
12. Rob Walker, "Martha Unwrapped," *Slate*, June 19, 2001.

13. "Martha Stewart Living Omnimedia, Inc., Announces Expansion of Its *Martha Stewart Baby Publication*," PR Newswire, February 20, 2001.
14. "Martha Stewart Living Keeps Sunny Outlook: Profits Up 25 Percent Despite Ad Softness, Economic Uncertainty," *National Post* (Canada), November 1, 2001.
15. Cathleen McGuigan, "Admiring Martha," *Newsweek*, April 18, 2002.
16. Ibid.
17. Constance L. Hays, "Martha Stewart Crucial to a Kmart Turnaround," *New York Times*, January 22, 2002.
18. Patricia Sellers, "It's (Not) a Good Thing," *Fortune*, February 4, 2002.

CHAPTER 7: A DIFFERENT KIND OF HOME

1. Keith Naughton, "More 'Ridiculousness': As If Questions About Insider Trading Weren't Enough, Now Martha Stewart Faces Inquiries About a Cover-Up," *Newsweek*, July 8, 2002.
2. Daniel Kadlec, "Sam's Club," *Time*, June 24, 2002.
3. Keith Naughton, "Martha's Tabloid Dish," *Newsweek*. June 24, 2002.
4. Naughton, "More 'Ridiculousness.'"
5. Keith Naughton, "More Head Wind for Martha," *Newsweek*, September 2, 2002.
6. Naughton, "More 'Ridiculousness.'"
7. Gloria Borger, "Why Hate Martha?" *U.S. News & World Report*, July 8, 2002.
8. Constance L. Hays and Tracie Rozhon, "Is There Life for Martha Stewart Living Omnimedia Without Martha?" *New York Times*, September 5, 2002.
9. Marianne Lavelle, "Time to Butter Up the Jury," *U.S. News & World Report*, January 26, 2004.
10. Alex Tresniowski, et. al., "A Fine Mess," *People Weekly*, September 23, 2002.
11. Tresniowski, et. al., "A Fine Mess,"
12. J.D. Heyman, "Pressure Cooker," *People Weekly*, June 23, 2003.
13. Keith Naughton, "Martha's Shrinking Act," *Newsweek*, November 4, 2002.
14. Tracie Rozhon, "The Undermining of the House of Stewart," *New York Times*, June 4, 2003.
15. Jyoti Thottam, "Why They're Picking on Martha," *Time*, June 16, 2003.
16. Peg Tyre and Daniel McGinn, "A Big House for Martha?" *Newsweek*, June 16, 2003.
17. Daniel Kadlec, "Not a Good Thing for Martha," *Time*, March 15, 2004.

18. Patricia Sellers, "Designing Her Defense," *Fortune*, June 23, 2003.
19. Heyman, "Pressure Cooker."
20. Ibid.
21. "A Sudden Smile," *People Weekly*, October 27, 2003.
22. Simon Crittle, "Why Is Martha Smiling?" *Time*, February 9, 2004.
23. Constance L. Hays, "Take Over for Martha Stewart? Her Daughter Says No Thanks," *New York Times*, March 17, 2004.
24. "A Glance at Martha Stewart's World," Associated Press, March 3, 2004.
25. Michael Brus, "The Fall of the House of Stewart," *Slate*, March 6, 2004.
26. Jill Smolowe, et. al., "A World Turned Upside Down," *People Weekly*, March 22, 2004.
27. Barney Gimbel, "Martha: Tell It to The Judge," *Newsweek*, March 29, 2004.
28. "Shopping for Support," *People Weekly*, April 5, 2004.
29. Ibid.
30. Ibid.
31. Sarah Karush, "Kmart Withdraws Suit Against Stewart," Associated Press Online, April 26, 2004.
32. Patricia Sellers, "Remodeling Martha," *Fortune*, November 14, 2005.
33. Patricia Sellers, "Martha's Team Has a Secret Plan," *Fortune*, April 19, 2004.
34. Keith Naughton, "Martha Holds Out a Helping Hand," *Newsweek*, June 7, 2004.
35. Jyoti Thottam, "Martha's Endgame," *Time*, July 26, 2004.
36. Keith Naughton, "I Will Be Back," *Newsweek*, July 26, 2004.
37. Ibid.
38. Simon Crittle, "No Decorating for a While," *Time*, July 26, 2004.
39. Bill Hewitt and Sharon Cotliar, "I'll Be Back," *People Weekly*, August 2, 2004.
40. Ibid.
41. Patricia Sellers, "Why Martha May Choose Jail Now," *Fortune*, August 9, 2004.
42. Greg Farrell and Theresa Howard, "Stewart Takes Steps to Reclaim 'Good Life,'" *USA Today*, September 15, 2004.
43. Richard Jerome, et. al., "Doing Her Time," *People Weekly*, October 25, 2004.
44. Ibid.
45. Lloyd Allen, *Being Martha: The Inside Story of Martha Stewart and Her Amazing Life*. Hoboken, N.J.: John Wiley & Sons, 2006, p. 184.

46. Sellers, "Remodeling Martha."
47. Winfrey, "Oprah's Cut with Martha Stewart."
48. Pam Lambert and Alicia C. Shepard, "Making Herself at Home," *People Weekly*, December 13, 2004.
49. Allen, *Being Martha*.
50. Alex Tresniowski and Sharon Cotliar, et. al., "She's Halfway Home," *People Weekly*, January 17, 2005.
51. Lambert and Shepard, "Making Herself at Home."
52. Tresniowski and Cotliar, et. al., "She's Halfway Home."
53. Alex Tresniowski and Alicia C. Shepard, et. al., "Martha's Moment," *People Weekly*, March 21, 2005.

CHAPTER 8: MARTHA STEWART'S REBIRTH

1. Keith Naughton, "Martha Breaks Out," *Newsweek*, March 7, 2005.
2. Tresniowski and Shepard, et. al., "Martha's Moment."
3. Jonathan Berr and Aimee Picchi, "Life Altering Experience," (Montreal) *Gazette*, March 5, 2005.
4. Carla Hay and Stephen M. Silverman, "Ellen DeGeneres Sweeps Daytime Emmy Awards," *People Weekly*, May 21, 2005.
5. Tresniowski and Shepard, et. al., "Martha's Moment."
6. Naughton, "Martha Breaks Out."
7. Ibid.
8. Anne D'Innocenzio, "Martha Stewart to Challenge SEC Insider Trading Charges," Associated Press, May 26, 2006.
9. "*Martha's Rules* by Martha Stewart to Be Published by Rodale in October 2005," PR Newswire, July 13, 2005.
10. Naughton, "Martha Breaks Out."
11. Trump, "The Domestic Diva Is Back."
12. Martha Stewart and Sharon Cotliar, "The 50 Most Beautiful People," *People Weekly*, May 9, 2005.
13. Berr and Picchi, "Life Altering Experience."
14. D'Innocenzio, "Martha Stewart to Challenge SEC Insider Trading Charges."
15. "Martha Stewart to Pay $5M to Settle ImClone Suit," Associated Press Worldstream, November 8, 2006.
16. Marc Peyser, "She's Back!" *Newsweek*, August 19, 2005.
17. Michele Orecklin, "10 Questions for Martha Stewart," *Time*, September 19, 2005.
18. "Ready for Prime Time," *People Weekly*, August 15, 2005.
19. Ibid.
20. Martha Stewart, "Martha's New Kitchen," *Martha Stewart Living*, September 2003.
21. "Ready for Prime Time."
22. Orecklin, "10 Questions for Martha Stewart."
23. Sellers, "Remodeling Martha."

24. Tom Van Riper, "Forbes 400 Drop-Offs," *Forbes*, September 19, 2007.
25. Sellers, "Remodeling Martha."
26. Ibid.
27. "Stewart to Market $15 Wine," *San Francisco Chronicle*, September 15, 2007.
28. "How Does She Do It All?" *Chicago Tribune*, July 29, 2007.
29. LaMotta, "Martha and Emeril: Cozy in the Kitchen."
30. Lisa McLaughlin, "On the Road with Martha Stewart," *Time*, April 23, 2007.
31. Jura Koncius, "It's Martha," *Washington Post*, September 13, 2007.
32. Martha Stewart, "From My Home to Yours: I Remember Mama," *Martha Stewart Living*, February 2008.
33. Martha Stewart, "The Martha Blogs: The Macy's Flower Show and Book Signing." Found at http://www.marthastewart.com, March 18, 2008.
34. Martha Stewart, "The Martha Blogs: Fun Photos of My Pets." Found at http://www.marthastewart.com, March 17, 2008.
35. Alice Short, "Martha Stewart Bids Paw Paw Farewell," *Los Angeles Times*, April 17, 2008.

BIBLIOGRAPHY

"A Dress Code Drama." *People Weekly*, June 28, 1999.

"A Glance at Martha Stewart's World." Associated Press, March 3, 2004.

"A Sudden Smile." *People Weekly*, October 27, 2003.

Allen, Lloyd. *Being Martha: The Inside Story of Martha Stewart and Her Amazing Life*. Hoboken, N.J.: John Wiley & Sons, 2006.

Beers, Charlotte, Martha Stewart, and Darla Moore. "Cocktails at Charlotte's with Martha and Darla." *Fortune*, August 5, 1996.

Berr, Jonathan, and Aimee Picchi. "Life Altering Experience." (Montreal) *Gazette*, March 5, 2005.

"Biography: Martha Stewart—Multimedia Lifestyle Entrepreneur." Academy of Achievement Web site. Available online at http://www.achievement.org/autodoc/page/ste0bio-1.

Borger, Gloria. "Why Hate Martha?" *U.S. News & World Report*, July 8, 2002.

Brown, Patricia Leigh. "The Perfect Wedding: Only Tears of Joy." *New York Times*, April 4, 1987.

Brus, Michael. "The Fall of the House of Stewart." *Slate*, March 6, 2004.

Carmody, Deirdre. "The Media Business: Martha Stewart Gains a Fan: Time Warner." *New York Times*, May 27, 1991.

Chesnoff, Richard Z. "The Real Joy of Cooking." *U.S. News & World Report*, September 25, 1995.

Crittle, Simon. "No Decorating for a While." *Time*, July 26, 2004.

———. "Why Is Martha Smiling?" *Time*, February 9, 2004.

DeRosa, Robin. "For Martha Stewart, Life Is for Nothing but 'Living.'" *USA Today*, December 15, 1993.

Didion, Joan. "Everywoman.com." *New Yorker*, February 21, 2000.

D'Innocenzio, Anne. "Martha Stewart to Challenge SEC Insider Trading Charges." Associated Press, May 26, 2006.

Donahue, Deirdre. "Stewart's Gold Touch." *USA Today*, December 18, 1989.

Farrell, Greg, and Theresa Howard. "Stewart Takes Steps to Reclaim 'Good Life.'" *USA Today*, September 15, 2004.

"Ford, Mercury Sign Martha Stewart Deal." *Automotive Age*, September 7, 1998.

Gerston, Jill. "Life Is Just a Bowl of Rhubarb Crisp (And So Easy!)." *New York Times*, October 9, 1994.

Gill, Brendan. "The Weekend House." *New Yorker*, October 16, 1995.

Gimbel, Barney. "Martha: Tell It to the Judge." *Newsweek*, March 29, 2004.

Graham, Renee. "Martha Stewart Shows Up (and on) 'Ellen.'" *Boston Globe*, November 15, 1995.

Green, Michelle. "The Best Revenge—for Martha Stewart, Living Well May Be Much, Much More Than a Vast Cottage Industry." *People Weekly*, October 2, 1995.

Hays, Constance L. "Martha Stewart Crucial to a Kmart Turnaround." *New York Times*, January 22, 2002.

———. "Take Over for Martha Stewart? Her Daughter Says No Thanks." *New York Times*, March 17, 2004.

Hays, Constance, and Tracie Rozhon. "Is There Life for Martha Stewart Living Omnimedia Without Martha?" *New York Times*, September 5, 2002.

Heffernan, Virginia. "Martha Makes Merry." *Slate*, December 5, 2002.

Hewitt, Bill, and Sharon Cotliar. "I'll Be Back." *People Weekly*, August 2, 2004.

Heyman, J.D. "Pressure Cooker." *People Weekly*, June 23, 2003.

Horn, Miriam. "Martha Stewart Living Large—Retailing." *U.S. News & World Report*, March 3, 1997.

"How Does She Do It All?" *Chicago Tribune*, July 29, 2007.

"Interview: Martha Stewart—Multimedia Lifestyle Entrepreneur." Academy of Achievement Web site, June 2, 1995. Available online at http://www.achievement.org/autodoc/page/ste0int-1.

Jerome, Richard, et. al. "Doing Her Time." *People Weekly*, October 25, 2004.

Kadlec, Daniel. "Not a Good Thing for Martha." *Time*, March 15, 2004.

Karush, Sarah. "Kmart Withdraws Suit Against Stewart." Associated Press Online, April 26, 2004.

Kelly, Keith J. "More Martha Stewart on TV Is OK'd." *Advertising Age*, August 26, 1996.

King, Angela K. "Right Time for Martha to Control Her Empire." *Daily News* (New York), February 5, 1997.

Koncius, Jura. "It's Martha." *Washington Post*, September 13, 2007.

LaMotta, Lisa. "Martha and Emeril: Cozy in the Kitchen." *Forbes*, February 19, 2008.

Lambert, Pam, and Alicia C. Shepard. "Making Herself at Home." *People Weekly*, December 13, 2004.

Lashinsky, Adam. "Managing Martha." *Fortune*, June 10, 2002.

Lavelle, Marianne. "Time to Butter Up the Jury." *U.S. News & World Report*, January 26, 2004.

Maker, Elizabeth. "Martha Stewart Tip: Feng Shui with Fur." *New York Times*, February 24, 2002.

Marin, Rick. "Be-Marthas, Do-Marthas, and Beyond Martha: Add a Christmas Special to Her Omnimedia Empire." *Newsweek*, December 11, 1995.

"Martha Stewart." Portfolio.com. Available online at http://www. portfolio.com/resources/executive-profiles/Martha-Stewart-25369.

"Martha Stewart." *People Weekly*, May 6, 1996.

"Martha Stewart Biography." FoxNews.com. Available online at http://www.foxnews.com/story/0,2933,193645,00.html?sPage=fnc/ entertainment/celebrity/stewart.

"Martha Stewart Gets TV Show." *Advertising Age*, January 25, 1993.

"*Martha Stewart Living* Keeps Sunny Outlook: Profits Up 25 Percent Despite Ad Softness, Economic Uncertainty." *National Post* (Canada), November 1, 2001.

"Martha Stewart Living Omnimedia, Inc., Announces Expansion of Its *Martha Stewart Baby* Publication." PR Newswire, February 20, 2001.

"Martha Stewart to Pay $5M to Settle ImClone Suit." Associated Press Worldstream, November 8, 2006.

"*Martha's Rules* by Martha Stewart to Be Published by Rodale in October 2005." PR Newswire US, July 13, 2005.

McGuigan, Cathleen. "Admiring Martha." *Newsweek*, April 18, 2002.

McLaughlin, Lisa. "On the Road with Martha Stewart." *Time*, April 23, 2007.

Naughton, Keith. "I Will Be Back." *Newsweek*, July 26, 2004.

———. "Martha Breaks Out." *Newsweek*, March 7, 2005.

———. "Martha Holds Out a Helping Hand." *Newsweek*, June 7, 2004.

———. "Martha's Shrinking Act." *Newsweek*, November 4, 2002.

———. "Martha's Tabloid Dish." *Newsweek*, June 24, 2002.

———. "More Head Wind for Martha." *Newsweek*, September 2, 2002.

———. "More 'Ridiculousness': As If Questions About Insider Trading Weren't Enough, Now Martha Stewart Faces Inquiries About a Cover-Up." *Newsweek*, July 8, 2002.

O'Neill, Anne-Marie, and Sue Miller. "Martha's Midas Touch." *People Weekly*, December 13, 1999.

Oppenheimer, Jerry. "The Imperfect Life of Miss Perfect." *Toronto Sun*, July 20, 1997.

Orecklin, Michele. "10 Questions for Martha Stewart." *Time*, September 19, 2005.

Peyser, Marc. "She's Back!" *Newsweek*, August 29, 2005.

Pogrebin, Robin. "Master of Her Own Destiny." *New York Times*, February 8, 1998.

"Ready for Prime Time." *People Weekly*, August 15, 2005.

Roach, Margaret. "Mother Knows Best." *Martha Stewart Living*, February 2004.

Rosenberg, Merri. "For Martha Stewart, a 152-Acre Estate in Katonah." *New York Times*, November 12, 2000.

Rozhon, Tracie. "The Undermining of the House of Stewart." *New York Times*, June 4, 2003.

Sellers, Patricia. "Designing Her Defense." *Fortune*, June 23, 2003.

———. "It's (Not) a Good Thing." *Fortune*, February 4, 2002.

———. "Martha's Team Has a Secret Plan." *Fortune*, April 19, 2003.

———. "Remodeling Martha." *Fortune*, November 14, 2005.

———. "Why Martha May Choose Jail Now." *Fortune*, August 9, 2004.

"Shopping for Support." *People Weekly*, April 5, 2004.

Short, Alice. "Martha Stewart Bids Paw Paw Farewell." *Los Angeles Times*, April 17, 2008.

Smolowe, Jill, et. al. "A World Turned Upside Down." *People Weekly*, March 22, 2004.

Stewart, Martha. "A Letter from Martha." *Martha Stewart Living*, December 1999.

———. *Christmas with Martha Stewart Living*. New York: Martha Stewart Living Omnimedia, 1997.

———. *Decorating for the Holidays*. New York: Martha Stewart Living Omnimedia, 1998.

———. *Entertaining*. New York: Clarkson Potter, 1982.

———. "From My Home to Yours: Summer's Best Flavor—Tomatoes." *Martha Stewart Living*, July 2005.

———. "From My Home to Yours: The First Fifteen Years." *Martha Stewart Living*, January 2006.

———. "The Martha Blogs: Fun Photos of My Pets." Found at http://www.marthastewart.com, March 17, 2008.

———. *Good Things*. New York: Martha Stewart Living Omnimedia, 1997.

———. "Martha's New Kitchen." *Martha Stewart Living*, September 2003.

———. *Martha Stewart's Quick Cook Menus*. New York: Clarkson Potter, 1988.

———. "Remembering." *Martha Stewart Living*, August 2002.

———. "Remembering." *Martha Stewart Living*, August 2003.

———. "Remembering." *Martha Stewart Living*, October 2002.

———. "Remembering: At Home with Big Martha." *Martha Stewart Living*, February 2008.

———. "Remembering: Cozy Comfort." *Martha Stewart Living*, January 2004.

———. "Remembering Turkey Hill." *Martha Stewart Living*, October 2007.

———. "The Martha Blogs: The Macy's Flower Show and Book Signing." Found at http://www.marthastewart.com, March 18, 2008.

Stewart, Martha, and Sharon Cotliar. "The 50 Most Beautiful People." *People Weekly*, May 9, 2005.

"Stewart to Market $15 Wine." *San Francisco Chronicle*, September 15, 2007.

Tajitsu, Naomi. "Martha Stewart Pinpoints Japanese Market." *The Daily Yomiuri* (Tokyo, Japan), November 18, 2000.

Thottam, Jyoti. "Martha's Endgame." *Time*, July 26, 2004.

———. "Why They're Picking on Martha." *Time*, June 16, 2003.

"Time 25: Time's 25 Most Influential Americans." *Time*, June 17, 1996.

Tresniowski, Alex, et. al. "A Fine Mess." *People Weekly*, September 23, 2002.

Tresniowski, Alex and Sharon Cotliar, et. al. "She's Halfway Home." *People Weekly*, January 17, 2005.

Tresniowski, Alex, and Alicia C. Shepard, et. al. "Martha's Moment." *People Weekly*, March 21, 2005.

Trump, Donald. "The Domestic Diva Is Back." *Time*, April 18, 2005.

Tyre, Peg. "Will Martha Make a Move?" *Newsweek*, January 28, 2002.

Tyre, Peg, and Daniel McGinn. "A Big House for Martha?" *Newsweek*, June 16, 2003.

Van Riper, Tom. "Forbes 400 Drop-Offs." *Forbes*, September 19, 2007.

Walker, Rob. "Martha Unwrapped." *Slate*, June 19, 2001.

Weir, June. "Taking Her Show on the Road: 'Queen of Home' Martha Stewart Looks to Interactive Media." *Advertising Age*, August 22, 1994.

Williams, Mary Elizabeth. "Salon Brilliant Careers: She's Martha and You're Not." *Salon*, February 1999.

Winfrey, Oprah. "Oprah's Cut with Martha Stewart." *O, the Oprah Magazine*, September 2000.

FURTHER RESOURCES

BOOKS

Adler, Bill. *The World According to Martha*. New York: McGraw-Hill, 2005.

Price, Joann F. *Martha Stewart: A Biography*. Westport, Conn.: Greenwood Press, 2007.

Slater, Bill. *Martha on Trial, in Jail, and on a Comeback*. Upper Saddle River, N.J.: FT Press, 2005.

Stewart, Martha. *The Martha Rules: Ten Essentials for Building Success as You Start, Build, or Manage a Business*. Emmaus, Pa.: Rodale Books, 2005.

———. *Martha Stewart's Cookies: The Very Best Treats to Bake and to Share*. New York: Martha Stewart Living Omnimedia, 2008.

———. *Martha Stewart's Cooking School: Lessons and Recipes for the Cook*. New York: Clarkson Potter, 2008.

WEB SITES

Academy of Achievement: Martha Stewart
http://www.achievement.org/autodoc/page/ste0pro-1

Court TV News: Martha Stewart Stock Scandal
http://www.courttv.com/trials/stewart

Martha Stewart
http://www.marthastewart.com

The Martha Stewart Show
http://www.marthastewart.com/affiliateinfo

PICTURE CREDITS

Page

10: AP Images

13: Time & Life Pictures/
    Getty Images

18: WireImage

23: AP Images

34: Getty Images

37: AP Images

42: Time & Life Pictures/
    Getty Images

47: Gerardo Somoza/Landov

51: © Tony Savino/Sygma/
    Corbis

58: Time & Life Pictures/
    Getty Images

62: AP Images

66: Getty Images

70: AP Images

77: CBS/Landov

82: AP Images

90: AP Images

93: AP Images

98: AP Images

102: Shannon Stapleton/
     Reuters/Landov

110: AP Images

INDEX

A

Alderson Federal Prison Camp
  time spent in, 14–15, 91–95,
    96, 100, 101
Apprentice: Martha Stewart, The
  (television show), 88, 99–100,
  103
  reviews for, 104
"Ask Martha" (radio spots), 61
*At Home with Martha Stewart
  This Christmas* (television special), 48

B

Baking with Julia (television
  program), 52
Bankhead, Tallulah, 44
Barnard College, 38
  education at, 8, 22, 24–27, 56
Bedford, New York
  farm in, 7, 67–68, 72, 79, 94,
    103, 105
  history, 72–73
  house arrest at, 87, 97
Beers, Charlotte, 56
Bernhardt Furniture, 86, 99
Blueprint (magazine), 105
Bolton, Michael, 44
Borger, Gloria, 79
Bunshaft, Gordon, 50
Burnett, Mark, 94, 98–99, 104
business
  branching out, 36, 41, 43,
    52, 56–57, 59, 105
  brand, 12, 14–15, 49, 59–60,
    71, 80, 84, 99, 105
  catering, 9, 32–35, 40, 49,
    61, 105, 111
  going public, 65–67, 69
  staff, 49–50, 53–54, 85–86,
    97, 111

C

Cedarbaum, Miriam,
  87

Child, Julia, 24–25
  cookbooks, 25, 26, 52
Child, Paul, 24–25
*Christmas with Martha Stewart
  Living* (book), 64
Clayson, Jane, 76
Clinton, Bill, 8
Columbia University, 8, 26, 28
cooking and entertaining,
    11–12, 35
  ethnic, 26, 27, 38, 39
  healthy eating, 52
  learning, 17, 20, 30, 64
  lessons, 31, 40
crafting, 11–12, 14, 43
Culinary Institute of America
  Hall of Fame, 25

D

Davis, Bette, 44
Decorating for the Holidays
  (book), 61
DeGeneres, Ellen, 52–53
Department of Justice, 75
Discovery Channel, 103
Dobbs, Lou, 82
Donahue, Phil, 44
Downey, James, 66
Dunne, Dominick, 87

E

Early Show, The, 67, 76, 78
East Hampton, New York
  houses in, 50, 67, 83
Ellen (sitcom), 52
Emeril (sitcom), 107
Emeril Green (television show),
  107
Emeril Lagasse Foundation,
  107
EMI Music, 88
Emmy Awards
  winners, 56, 98, 104
Entertaining (book), 26
  anniversary of, 10–11, 105

childhood foods in, 19, 20, 22
popularity of, 36–37
publication of, 9–12, 35, 49
writing of, 34
Essence of Emeril (television show), 106–107
Estée Lauder cosmetics company, 100

F

Federal Bureau of Investigation, 75
Fitzgerald, F. Scott
   The Great Gatsby, 44
Food and Drug Administration, 76–77
Forbes magazine, 67, 104
Ford Motor Company, 60
Fortune magazine, 9, 56, 74, 104
French Chef, The (television show), 25

G

gardening, 85
   love of, 17–18, 30, 32–33, 41, 64
Gates, Bill, 62
Gehry, Frank, 53
Good Morning America (television show), 25
Good Things (book), 59
Great Depression, 20
Great Gatsby, The (Fitzgerald), 44
Grubman, Allen, 49
Gumbel, Bryant, 67

H

Heffernan, Virginia, 15
Home for Holidays (television special), 56
Hors d'Oeurves (cookbook), 36
House Beautiful magazine
   articles for, 12, 36

I

ImClone stock, 75–78
investigation into stock sale, 14
   appeals, 85
   details of, 75–81
   indictment, 81–83
   sentencing, 87–91
   support during, 79–80, 86, 100
   and trial, 83–85
Is Martha Stewart Living? (calendar), 53, 66

J

Jackson, Michael, 86, 89
Jay, John, 73

K

KB Home, 15, 105
King, Larry, 83
Klein, Calvin, 91
Kmart, 94
   commercials for, 41
   financial problems, 74, 78
   lawsuit, 84, 86
   products for, 12, 36, 59, 62, 74, 84, 86, 99
   royalties, 57
Koppelman, Charles, 88–89
   reshaping images, 86–87, 88–89
Kostyra, Eddie (father), 16, 19, 20
   gardening, 17–18
Kostyra, Eric (brother), 16, 18
Kostyra, Frank (brother), 16
Kostyra, George (brother), 16
Kostyra, Kathy (sister), 16, 19
Kostyra, Laura (sister), 16
Kostyra, Martha (mother), 16, 20, 26, 83, 84, 93
   childhood, 17
   cooking, 17, 19, 21, 64, 108
   death, 108–109

L

Lagasse, Emeril, 106–107
  brand, 12, 15, 105, 106–107
Lauren, Ralph, 9, 62, 65
Le Cordon Bleu cooking
  school, 25
lectures and seminars, 12, 40,
  48
Letterman, David, 53
Lifetime network, 36, 48
Lindbergh, Charles, 44
Lyne, Susan, 99–100

M

Macy's
  products for, 12, 15, 105,
    107–108
Madden, Steve, 86, 88
Madonna, 49
Martha, Inc. (book and TV
  movie), 80
Martha Rules, The (book), 99,
  104
Martha Stewart Baby (magazine),
  71, 84
Martha Stewart Kids (magazine),
  84
Martha Stewart Living (magazine), 54, 60, 80, 91
  advertisers, 71, 100, 104
  "Ask Martha" section, 70
  awards for, 56
  childhood memories in, 8,
    17–19
  homes in, 32, 46, 48
  launch of, 13, 46, 48
  success of, 48, 56, 67, 71,
    84
Martha Stewart Living radio
  channel, 99
Martha Stewart Living (television show), 85
  awards for, 56, 98
  debut, 48
  filming of, 13, 48, 61

sponsor, 60
  success of, 60–61, 84
  topics on, 48–49
Martha Stewart Living Enterprises
  annual revenues of, 57
  creation of, 56
Martha Stewart Living Omnimedia, 80, 84, 94, 105
  advertisers, 60
  board, 88, 99–100
  creation of, 57
  employees, 67, 97
  stocks, 65–66, 68–69, 78, 80,
    99, 104
Martha Stewart Living Omnimedia Foundation, 111
Martha Stewart Show, The (talk
  show), 10, 104, 105, 108, 111
  500th episode, 7–8
  developing, 15, 99, 101, 103
Martha Stewart's Cakes (cookbook), 109
Martha Stewart's Christmas
  (book), 41–42
Martha Stewart's Cookies (cookbook), 109
*Martha Stewart's Healthy Quick
  Cook* (cookbook), 61
Martha Stewart's Quick Cook
  (cookbook), 36
*Martha Stewart's Quick Cook
  Menus* (cookbook), 18, 38
Martha Stewart Vintage, 105
Martha Stewart Wedding Invi-
  tation Collection, 43
Martha Stewart Weddings (maga-
  zine), 67, 71, 84
*Mastering the Art of French Cook-
  ing* (Child), 25, 26, 52
McGuigan, Cathleen, 72–73
McNeil, Leslie, 13
modeling career, 22, 25, 27
Monness, Andy, 9, 28–29
Museum of Modern Art, 50

N

Nash, Daniel, 45
Newman, Paul, 44–45
Newsweek, 11, 54, 73, 78
New York Stock Exchange, 65,
    68–69, 77
New York Times, The, 11, 12, 57,
    67
    articles in, 13, 36, 38, 50, 70,
        79, 81
    bestseller list, 41, 104
Nutley, New Jersey, 83
    growing up in, 16–20, 21–22

O

O'Brien, Conan, 8, 109
O'Donnell, Rosie, 83
Ogilvy & Mather, 56

P

Patrick, Sharon, 81–82, 99
People Weekly
    articles, 52, 55, 83, 86, 92,
        98–99, 100
Picasso, Pablo, 9
Picasso, Paloma, 9
Pies and Tarts (cookbook), 36
Pittman, Sandy Hill, 54
Prudhomme, Paul, 38

S

Saugatuck River, 44
SaveMartha.com, 79
Scott, Walter, 22
Seal Harbor, Maine, 67
Sears, Roebuck & Co., 62, 94
Securities and Exchange Com-
    mission, 75, 101
Sedaka, Neil, 44
Seinfeld, Jerry, 53
September 11, 2001, terrorist
    attacks, 71
Serling, Rod, 44
Sinatra, Frank, 89
Sirius Satellite Radio, 99, 103

Smith College, 24
Stewart, Alexis (daughter), 38,
    41, 50, 96–97
    childhood, 9, 27, 28–29, 31
    on television, 88
    and the trial, 81, 83–84, 87,
        89
    visiting jail, 91–92
    yoga, 100
Stewart, Andy (husband)
    divorce, 14, 41, 50
    marriage, 8–9, 14, 26, 29
    travels, 26–27
    Turkey Hill, 30–31, 32, 41,
        46
Stewart, Martha
    childhood, 8, 16–22
    chronology, 112–113
    criticism of, 14, 43, 53, 59,
        66, 100, 104–105
    divorce, 14, 41, 50
    education, 8, 22–27, 56
    marriage, 8–9, 14, 26, 29
    modeling career, 22, 25,
        27
    net worth, 8
    perfectionist, 35, 42–43, 71
    reading, 11, 21–22
    and sleep, 11, 12, 42, 49
    as stockbroker, 9, 28–30
    travels, 26–27, 54
Stockton, Frank, 21
Stowe, Harriet Beecher, 21

T

Taylor, Elizabeth, 44
There's a Chef in My Soup
    (Lagasse), 107
This Morning, 60
Thomas, Marlo, 44
Time Inc.
    relationship with, 56–57
Time magazine, 11
    articles, 35, 53, 100, 103,
        107

Today show
  appearances on, 36, 39, 48,
    57
Tolstoy, Leo, 22
Trump, Donald, 35, 88, 100,
  104
Turkey Hill, 50, 67, 84
  photos of, 33, 46, 48
  renovation of, 30–31, 32, 41,
    46
  sale of, 33
  seminars at, 12, 40
  on television, 33, 41, 61

U
Ubben, Jeff, 81
USA Today, 39, 43, 48
U.S. News & World Report, 79

V
Vanilla Ice, 89

W
Waksal, Sam, 76

Wall Street
  stockbroker on, 9, 28–30
Wall Street Journal, The, 11
Washington Post, The, 108
Wedding Planner, The (book), 38
Weddings (book), 36–38
Westport, Connecticut
  catering business in, 9, 32–33,
    35, 40, 49, 59, 111
  history of, 44–45
  home in, 9, 12–13, 30–33,
    40–41, 46, 48, 61–62, 67, 83
Wharton, Edith, 22
Williams, Mary Elizabeth, 22
Willis, Virginia, 111
Winfrey, Oprah, 22, 53, 92
Woodward, Joanne, 44–45
Wyland, Susan, 48, 54

Z
Zucker, Jeff, 99

ABOUT THE AUTHOR

SHERRY BECK PAPROCKI has written or contributed to eight books for children. *Oprah Winfrey, Talk Show Host and Media Magnate* (Infobase Publishing, 2006) earned a spot on the 2006 Nonfiction Honor List created by the Voice of Youth Advocates (VOYA). In addition, she has written *Katie Couric* (Chelsea House, 2001), *Michelle Kwan* (Chelsea House, 2001), and several other books. She is the editor of *Columbus Monthly Homes* in Ohio, and her bylines have appeared in *Preservation* magazine, *The Chicago Tribune*, the *Cleveland Plain Dealer, The Philadelphia Inquirer*, the Los Angeles Times Syndicate, and many other publications. She is a graduate of The Ohio State University School of Journalism and resides near Columbus, Ohio, where she also serves as an adjunct faculty member of Otterbein College. She and her husband, Ray, are the parents of two adult children—Justin and Ana Paprocki.